P9-BXY-529

Praise for *Wake Up America!*

"Here Tony Campolo, activist extraordinary and visionary motivator, opens his mind and heart on aspects of the spiritual renewal that America needs. Perceiving that true revival has feet, he maps out paths of neighbor-love along which quickened Christians should be walking today. One need not agree with all his opinions to find profound instruction and challenge in these pages."

—James Packer, author of *Knowing God*

"Anything Tony Campolo writes is not just inviting . . . it is compelling—irresistible! *Wake Up America* is no exception.

"This is classic Campolo. With his unique, sensitive, humorous way, Tony reminds the people of God that to take Christ seriously is to be concerned and involved with human need of every kind. He reminds us on nearly every page that Christ is thirsty, naked, sick, and in prison. And we minister to Him when we minister to 'the least of these' who are in such need.

"Tony Campolo inspires not only with his simple, tough, caring style but with specific example after example in city after city where the Christ-like response to human need is being emulated.

"This book is the right one in the right way at the right time."

—Richard C. Halverson, chaplain,
United States Senate

"Keen analysis coupled with solid remedy—that is the remarkable combination which Campolo offers Christ's people in this book. Nothing I have read matches it in inspiration and instruction for the tasks that challenge America's churches and the good that will come if we rise to that challenge in the grace and power of God."

—David Hubbard, president, Fuller Theological Seminary

"I used to pray that God would mellow Tony. Now I pray that God will *move me*—and He often does through Tony's books and this is one of them!"

—Bill Hybels, author of *Honest to God*

"Tony Campolo's latest book *Wake Up America!* is a penetrating diagnosis of the sickness of the soul of our culture and an urgent call for an authentic spiritual awakening that leads to obedient discipleship. This book is solidly biblical and a bracing analysis of what it means to run with the Master on a two-legged gospel of personal commitment and compassionate mission. Campolo calls for a new breed of Christians who are faithful to changing the world by the power of the Spirit and who go all the way in living out the mandates of the Kingdom. After the equivocation of the epistles, here's a bracing, challenging book to help Christians and churches to confront the vacillation of the nineties."

—Lloyd John Ogilvie, pastor, The First Presbyterian Church of Hollywood

"We are used to having Tony Campolo make us laugh. But in this book he sounds like the prophet Amos. Read it! It's a matter of life and death."

—Bruce Larson, author of *Living Beyond Our Fears*

"Tony Campolo has captured some of the important issues that have crippled the foundation of America . . . [and] made Americans lonely and unsatisfied with life. Tony's book will help [us] come to grips with our souls and emotions to change our behavior for a better tomorrow."

—Matthew Parker, president, Institute for Black Family Development

"Tony Campolo's book *Wake Up America!* is a must to read. He puts his finger on the great issue of today, and that is materialistic idolatry. It has been woven into our whole American culture, and I agree with Tony when he says that we have found a way to meet our spiritual needs within our consumerism and materialism. It is a part of what we have become. In reality, we have tied the prosperity of our nation into consumptive materialism, and have deified that and reinforced it with a theology of prosperity.

"I further agree that in the midst of this, there is a ray of hope, and that hope is in God's people becoming the church at the community level, demonstrating that hope in a local neighborhood, but offering themselves and their service to the world.

"I believe that *Wake Up America!* could become one of the most important books of our time."

—John M. Perkins, president of the John Perkins Foundation, Pasadena, CA

"A powerful plea to transcend cultural Christianity and embrace costly discipleship. Classic Campolo—provocative, probing, powerful."

—Ron Sider, executive director, Evangelicals for Social Action, and professor of Theology & Culture, Eastern Baptist Theological Seminary

"Tony has escaped from the manacles of evangelical orthodoxy and has entered the promised land of the Word. His challenge resonates with the profundity of Amos, the empathy of Jeremiah, the hope of Ezekiel, and the compassion of Naomi. Sojourner Truth would be as proud of Campolo as she would of a natural son. No serious Christian can engage his proclamation without feeling a sense of urgency. If total spiritual holocaust is averted in our land, Tony Campolo will no doubt be listed among the heralds whose prophetic utterance awakened us from the comfort of our sleep."

—Buster Soaries, pastor, First Baptist Church of Lincoln Gardens, Somerset, NJ

"A powerful, prophetic message for America in the 1990s. A must-read for all followers of Jesus."

—Ruth A. Tucker, visiting professor at Trinity Evangelical Divinity School

"Tony Campolo is too funny to fit the usual stereotype of a prophet. But he certainly says prophetic things that the church needs to listen to. And in this book he takes the further, more difficult step of pointing to examples of people who are doing it right."

—Philip Yancey, author of *Disappointment With God*

WAKE UP
AMERICA!

Other Books by Tony Campolo

THE KINGDOM OF GOD IS A PARTY

THINGS WE WISH WE HAD SAID,
REFLECTIONS OF A FATHER AND HIS GROWN SON

GROWING UP IN AMERICA

20 HOT POTATOES
CHRISTIANS ARE AFRIAD TO TOUCH

SEVEN DEADLY SINS

WHO SWITCHED THE PRICE TAGS?

PARTLY RIGHT:
CHRISTIANITY RESPONDS TO ITS CRITICS

IT'S FRIDAY, BUT SUNDAY'S COMIN'

YOU CAN MAKE A DIFFERENCE

THE POWER DELUSION

A REASONABLE FAITH:
RESPONDING TO SECULARISM

IDEAS FOR SOCIAL ACTION: A HANDBOOK ON
MISSION AND SERVICE FOR YOUNG PEOPLE

THE SUCCESS FANTASY

A DENOMINATION LOOKS AT ITSELF

WAKE UP AMERICA!

ANSWERING GOD'S RADICAL CALL WHILE LIVING IN THE REAL WORLD

Tony Campolo

HarperSanFrancisco
ZondervanPublishingHouse
Divisions of HarperCollins*Publishers*

Grateful acknowledgment is made for use of the following:
"Class of '57" by Harold Reid and Don Reid, © 1972 by House of Cash,
Inc. (BMI). Administered by CMI, Nashville, TN. All rights reserved.
Used by permission. "How Great Thou Art," © 1953 by Manna Music,
Inc. International copyright secured. All rights reserved. Used by per-
mission.

All Scripture quotations in this publication are from the Holy Bible,
King James Version.

WAKE UP AMERICA!: *Answering God's Radical Call While Living in the
Real World.* Copyright © 1991 by Tony Campolo. All rights reserved.
Printed in the United States of America. No part of this book may be
used or reproduced in any manner whatsoever without written permission except in the case of brief quotations embodied in critical articles
and reviews. For information address HarperCollins Publishers, 10 East
53rd Street, New York, NY 10022.

Library of Congress Cataloging-in-Publication Data

Campolo, Anthony
    Wake up America! / Tony Campolo.
        p.   cm.
    Includes bibliographical references.
    ISBN 0–06–061302–5 (alk. paper)
    1. United States—Religious life and customs. 2. United States—Moral
    conditions. I. Title.
    [BR526.C35 1991]
    277.3'0829—dc20   89–45933
                                                               CIP

91 92 93 94 95 HAD 10 9 8 7 6 5 4 3

This edition is printed on acid-free paper that meets the American National
Standards Institute Z39.48 Standard.

To Dick Lane
A model for those who want to know
what a great Christian looks like

84966

CONTENTS

PREFACE

THIS HAS BEEN A HARD BOOK to write because it is filled with emotion. My future and the future of my country are wrapped up in its message. As I wrote it, I was forced to endure painful examination of both myself and the other people on this planet that I call my own. What I discovered is that I am part of a dying nation and of a people who have lost their dreams and visions.

But this is also a book filled with hope. I believe that a new breed of Christians with a new way of impacting the world is coming to center stage. And this new breed of Christians, I am convinced, is going to breathe new life into those dry bones called America.

No earthly being needs to give birth to this movement of renewal. The Lord Himself is making it happen. The new America is already among us as mustard seeds, and soon the fruit will be evident. It will not come in violent revolutions, which, in the end, do little except to change the palace guard. It will not come from political action that is designed to change things from the top down. Instead, it will come from a new breed of Christians working locally in programs and projects that separately and to the outside observer will not seem like much. But look again, because in what I call the "middle-range" activities, a new America will begin to flex its muscles and it will get up and walk around.

But before I get into my story, let me acknowledge the people who helped me get it together and into print. There is Mary Noel Keough, who made sure the manuscript got edited and typed. And there are Amy Kay Watson and Patricia Carroll, who actually did a lot of the typing. There is Lonnie Hull, the editor from HarperSanFrancisco who made me rethink what I had to say and how I would say it. And then there is the real partner in this mission—Peggy, my wife. People always ask, "Do you really write all of those books?" The answer is, "No! She does!" At least she sees to it that they get written right.

—*Tony Campolo*

INTRODUCTION

LATE ONE AFTERNOON I received a phone call from my friend John Bernbaum of the Christian College Coalition. He told me that a group of top educators from the Soviet Union were coming to the United States. The group included the rectors of two of the most prestigious universities of the USSR as well as the Russian Deputy Minister of Education. John explained that they were interested in seeing the things religious groups here in the United States are doing in the way of social service. Since I head an organization that has a variety of inner-city ministries in the greater Philadelphia area, John thought it would be a good thing for these Russians to see our work. I was pleased to have the opportunity to show off what my staff was accomplishing, so I readily agreed to the visit.

When the Russians arrived, they seemed impressed. With great enthusiasm I took them to our various latchkey programs. I showed off our youth clubs and explained how we communicate Christian values to ghetto teenagers. Finally, I took them to a special Christian school that we have established for disadvantaged children.

Everywhere these Russian visitors went they interviewed people—children and teenagers as well as adults. Their questions were probing and astute. They listened with intensity and they took copious notes.

At the end of the day we had a debriefing time, and I asked my guests about the impressions they had gained from the day's experiences. Their responses surprised me. "These teenagers are so materialistic!" was one response. Another added, "All that these young people talked about was making money." But the most unexpected answer came from the Deputy Minister of Education, who reluctantly remarked, "I am somewhat disappointed in your children. Since they are Christians, I expected that they would be concerned about spiritual things. Instead, they are more materialistic than the Marxist youth in my country. They seem to be devoid of any lofty, idealistic vision."

These responses were not what I had expected to hear. Seeing "Christian" children through the eyes of people from other countries provided something of a surprise, especially in light of the fact that these people who had pointed out the materialism of our youth were Marxists.

I asked myself if Christian kids in America have always been this way, or if this evident materialism and lack of spirituality is a recent development. I wondered if I had been like these kids when I was a teenager, or if something had died in the psyche of American youth since those days. And I asked myself if only teenagers were this way, or if all of us had changed during the last few decades.

Has the spirit of idealism departed from our collective consciousness without our being aware of it? Can it be that, in an era when religion has become one of the most prominent features of our culture, we Americans have lost our guiding inner light and lofty calling? And if we have become a people of dry bones, can these dry bones ever rise up and walk again?

This book is about such questions. Together, I want us to talk about the spiritual condition of America and to examine what has been happening to us over the last few decades. As you might surmise from the tone of these opening paragraphs, I do not think that the diagnosis will be good. I have to admit that I sense that something has been lost to America. I have a feeling that the sacredness of our national character has been "slip slidin' away."

But there is something else we must look at. There is a strange and mysterious force at work in our world. I can feel it, and most people with whom I talk can feel it too. It is a force that evidences itself in subtle ways in the music on Broadway and in the paintings of Andrew Wyeth. It is an intangible reality that lies just beneath the surface of the yuppie consciousness and is waiting to be born.

This force is nothing less than a spirit that will give birth to a new and different America with a new and different faith. It has a dynamism that has the wherewithal to sweep away the encroaching lethargy that seems to beset us on every side. It has an idealism that can coun-

teract the cynicism that has been eating away at our collective soul. It is a spirit that, in the words of the Apostle
Paul, is "with us, and in us," struggling to take form and
to fan the dying embers called America back to life
again. It is a spirit that will overcome the feeling that
America is living at the beginning of the end and will
make us believe that, in reality, we are facing a new
beginning.

This book is not only about what we have lost. It is
also about the "new thing" that God is doing in our
midst, and it is an invitation for you to be a part of it. It
is about the rebirth of a red-hot movement of the spirit
that stands against the cold death wish that hitherto has
haunted our souls and generated anxiety about our
future. I hope you will come away from reading this
book convinced that God has not given up on America
and that He is even now calling you to join Him in making our society radically new.

CHAPTER 1

HOW DID WE GET SO GOOD AT BEING SO BAD?

THIS IS NOT THE FIRST book to begin with the famous Dickens quote, "It was the best of times; it was the worst of times." But few quotes so aptly describe the end of the twentieth century. It is a time of brilliant technological achievement; but it also is a time when technology has overwhelmed us with problems. It is a time when it has at last become possible to produce enough food for everyone on the planet; but it also is a time when political and economic barriers have prevented food from getting to millions who live on the verge of starvation. It is a time when "the good life" seems within the grasp of so many; and yet it is a time when more people live in a narcissistic hell than most of us can imagine.

For those of us who live in the Western nations, the end of the twentieth century has been a time of triumph. Our political philosophy has swept away its opposition. The liberal democratic ideals born out of the Enlightenment and tested in the crucibles of the American and French Revolutions have won out over the threats of fascism on the one hand and communism on the other, and the values of the Constitution and the Declaration of Independence have become ideals for the entire world.

This victory of Western capitalism has come from neither military conquest nor rational debate. Instead, it has come from something much less dramatic or noble. It has triumphed by virtue of the fact that our socioeconomic system has been able to produce more consumer goods than any other. Consequently, our way of life has become not only the most desirable in the world but apparently, to most people, the only viable one. In the end, it is because democratic capitalism has produced more things for more people than any of its competitors that its reign has gained sway over the minds of most of humanity. It has delivered more decent housing, more automobiles, more home appliances, more designer jeans, more television sets, and more gourmet foods than anyone had hitherto dreamed possible.

Living in the "free world" has become synonymous with having consumer goods. This is what our system is all about. And when at last the hideous Berlin Wall came tumbling down, it was these consumer goods produced under the auspices of our social system that the people from the Eastern Bloc nations rushed in to grab. As one expatriate from East Germany so eloquently said, "We came! We saw! We shopped!" At the end of the twentieth century, democratic capitalism has created the greatest society of consumer goods ever known to the human race, and against that fact no ideological doctrine supporting an alternative system seems to stand a chance.

"It cannot be as simple at that," some will say. "People will not be satisfied with consumer goods alone. There must be deep spiritual reasons why democratic capitalism has won." Antimaterialistic pulpiteers rant on, claiming that if that is all there is to the triumph of our way of life, then it will not last. "People need homes, not just houses," they say. "They need love, not just things. They need meaning, not just entertainment."

Spiritual Gratification Through Material Means

What the would-be spiritual oracles fail to understand about our "advanced" capitalist social system is that the means have been devised to make spiritual realities somewhat unreal to most of us. More accurately, ways have been found in our consumer-oriented society to reduce spiritual hungers to emotions that can be gratified by purchasing the things being sold to us through the mass media. The tension between the spiritual and the material spheres of life increasingly is being overcome. In the context of our new social order, we more and more are being led to believe that our deepest spiritual needs, the sorts of realities that the Bible talks about, can be met simply by buying the right consumer goods.

If such assertions seem absurd, then consider how so many of the advertisements on television promise to deliver to us the blessings that, upon reflection, we once supposed could come only from right relationships with

God and with our neighbors. Consider how the popular media are now overcoming differences that once existed between the satisfactions provided by spiritual well-being and the satisfactions that come from consumer goods.

For instance, Coca Cola (in what may be the most famous television ad of all time) replicates the Biblical imagery of the Day of Pentecost. In the ad, people from various ethnic groups from around the world are assembled on a hilltop, holding hands and singing:

> I want to teach the world to sing
> in perfect harmony....

But what creates this perfect harmony for broken humanity, overcomes the curse of Babel, unifies us, and overcomes our sense of separateness is not the Holy Spirit. It's Coca Cola! For America, Coke has become "The Real Thing."

Or think about the way that the intimacy of Biblical *koinonia* (fellowship) supposedly can be generated simply by buying the right kind of beer. In a now-famous ad, we are invited to be the unseen guests of some sportsmen who are having a cookout on the back porch of a rustic lodge. They have just finished a good day of fishing and are cooking some of their catch. As they pull the tops off Lowenbrau beer cans, one of them comments, "It just doesn't get any better that this." Then, as the camera pulls back to give us a good overall view of the idyllic scene, a deep baritone voice sings out,

> Here's to good friends
> tonight is kind of special....

Through this ad, the viewers are being told that this beer will deliver far more than what is in the can. We are being told that Lowenbrau can overcome the loneliness of the soul.

In our TV ads, it is as though the ecstasy of the spirit experienced by a St. Theresa or a St. Francis can be reduced to the gratification coming from a particular car, and the kind of love that Christ compared to His love for His church can be expressed by buying the right kind of wristwatch "for that special person in your life." In all of this media hype, things are sold to us on the basis that our deepest emotional and psychological needs will be met by having the right consumer goods.

Hitherto, spiritual gratification could come only via spiritual means. Thus, people were urged to choose between the things of this world and the blessings of God. Now, that duality has been overcome. Ours is an age in which spiritual blessings are being promised to those who buy material things. The spiritual is being absorbed by the physical. The fruit of the spirit, suggests the media, can be had without God and without spiritual disciplines. It is not simply that we are materialists who crave the goods that flood our markets, but that we are now a people who subconsciously have been made to believe that in these things we will find an end to the spiritual longings at the ground of our being.

Perhaps the most evil consequence of selling consumer goods in this manner is that people like us no longer know what spiritual longings really are. We have become alienated from our real needs. Spiritual longings, which most of us can no longer even define, have come to be so identified with consumer goods that these consumer goods have taken on a quality of ultimateness for us.

But there is a catch in all of this. We sense that as the ads play up the theme of friendship, our loneliness becomes more acute. As the psychic ecstasy is played out on the electronic screen, our feelings of being hollow and empty become more severe. Those of us who long for love become more conscious of our plight as love seems to come so easily to those who buy the right things. These same processes are at work in ad themes ranging from self-worth to feeling free to define one's own destiny. The ads only increase our awareness of what is missing from our lives. They only heighten our consciousness of discontent.

When they have finished practicing their magic on us, the ads are really capable only of getting us to spend our money, while leaving us estranged from ourselves. We think it is the things that we want. We have forgotten that the spiritual blessings that the ads have associated with the things are really the desires of our hearts.

You would think that sooner or later we would see through these not-too-subtle deceptions. But thirsty people want to believe in their mirages. We want the ads to be true. And wishes can keep deceptions alive for a long, long time.

Even when the things depicted in the ads fail to deliver what the ads promise, we do not grasp the nature of the deception. There are always *new* ads that tell us of *new* things that have just been invented. These new things, they claim, will give us the "full satisfaction" we crave, even if the things previously advertised left us disappointed. The new products, we are told, will really do the trick if we will just give them a try. And so we go on and on, buying more and more, and all the time feeling less and less satisfied with life.

How Necessary is the False Consciousness Created by Ads?

Is all of this psychological manipulation really necessary? Does our economy really require the spiritual deception that lies behind so much of what we see and hear through the media? Has it really become necessary for us to have our minds seduced by images of consumer goods that supposedly provide us with everything from peace of mind to loving relationships?

Unfortunately, the answer to all of these questions is, "Yes!" Without the ads we wouldn't buy what we have to buy to keep America going. The American industrial machine has become so efficient that its people are not able to purchase all the things that it can produce. But if we are to keep Americans employed, that is exactly what we have to do. Buying American is essential if our workers are to have jobs.

Unfortunately, (or fortunately; I am not convinced which) most Americans already have everything they need. At least that is true for the people who have money to spend. Those of us who do have money can think of little that we need that we do not already have. We need no better evidence of that than Christmas, when our most serious problem is not how to get enough money to buy presents but what to buy for friends and relatives who have "everything."

When faced with the task of trying to get us to buy what we do not need in ever-increasing quantities, the ad people are left with no alternative except to pretend that the things they are selling will meet spiritual and psychological needs. That is why the ads take the form that they do. That is why material consumer goods are sold to us on the basis that they will meet our deeply felt needs for community, friendship, sexual identity, self-worth, love, and peace of mind.

We ought to think twice before we condemn these Madison Avenue wizards who get us to buy what we do not need. What would we Americans do without them? Such absurdity is what our society is all about.

Enslavement to Alienation

Among the many side effects of the commercial process is, according to the late Herbert Marcuse, a tendency to think that the artificially created wants (i.e., consumer goods) generated by ads are more essential to our well-being than the meeting of the real needs that go with being human.

Marcuse went on to explain that this commercial system has so permeated our consciousness that we are now caught up in a comfortable, attractive, pleasant form of slavery. And it is the worst kind of slavery, because freedom from it becomes nearly impossible. We would never consider rebelling against a social system that gives us what we *think* we want.

When Phil and Cynthia got married they were sure that they would create the perfect family. They had idyllic images of living in a rustic house in the woods, sitting with their children in front of a fireplace on Christmas Eve. They thought of the long walks and talks they would have, and the deep sense of sharing that would be theirs. Well, it didn't happen. And just after Christmas, Phil and Cynthia filed for a divorce. The disintegration of their marriage was the inevitable consequence of being enslaved to "the system."

At first, things seemed to go well. Phil worked as an insurance salesman and apparently made a decent living. Cynthia became a school teacher and very much enjoyed her work. But as the two of them tried to get themselves situated, it appeared to them that they needed more money than they were making between them. They just didn't seem to be able to buy all the things that they thought they needed.

The problem seemed easy enough to solve. That was what Phil liked about selling insurance. If you needed more money, all you had to do was to work a little harder, make a few extra calls on possible clients, and go to a few more sales conferences to improve your skills and to jack up motivation. There would be less time for those long walks and for the "sharings," but a guy's got to do what a guy's got to do. At least, that's what he told himself.

When the baby came, Phil and Cynthia were in a quandary. Of course they wanted the baby, but they also needed the money that came from Cynthia's teaching. The solution to the dilemma seemed to be day-care. Cynthia wouldn't be there to see little Jonathan take his first steps, and at times her little boy seemed to have more of a liking for his day-care attendant than for her, but then one has to make sacrifices if one is to provide a child with the things he needs. At least, that's what she told herself.

As time slipped by, something died in their marriage. Phil was always too tired and always had too little time to empathize with Cynthia. Cynthia ended up doing most of the housework and became exhausted feeding a small child, putting him to bed, and, of course, shopping for all the things he needed. It was no wonder that Phil and Cynthia always seemed a bit on edge and often gave curt answers to each other, but they had all the things they thought they needed. And besides, they were providing a good home for Jonathan. At least, that's what they told themselves.

This past Christmas things came to a head. Christmas has a way of bringing out people's problems. I suppose it is because Christmas embodies so many memories of what used to be and calls forth recollections of what was hoped would be. Whatever the reasons, Christmas was such a hollow, empty day that it revealed what Phil and Cynthia long had suspected. Their marriage was not a marriage at all.

These are the consequences of the kinds of sacrifices that people make in order to get the money they have to have to buy the things that they don't need for people who have everything. This is the kind of unconscious slavery that Marcuse was talking about. Phil and Cynthia thought that they were free, but they had been manipulated into enslavement to the things that "the system" had made ultimately important to them. Yet it is in the throes of this time of triumph that the liberal democratic capitalistic society we have created faces its greatest threat and challenge. The threat is not posed by anything external. It is not a challenge that arises from the menace of some totalitarian dictator or belligerent nuclear power or the terrorism promoted by a few Muslim fanatics that jeopardize our golden age and our optimism about the future.

Something Has Died in America

It is not just Phil and Cynthia that have got me worried. Something has happened to all of us spiritually. Putting it in Biblical language, it seems as though America itself has lost its soul. Something about our collective psyche has died. Apathy and numbness appear to have crept into our shared consciousness. And no amount of flag waving, jingoistic preaching, or nationalistic crusading has the potential for resurrecting our fading *volksgeist* to life again.

As I watched American sports fans shouting, "We're Number One!" at the 1984 Los Angeles Olympics, it had the sound of a last hurrah. Down deep inside, there was a gnawing sense that our Humpty Dumpty society had had a great fall and, even worse, a feeling that all the king's horses and all the king's men would not be able to put it together again. I don't know why it hit me at that moment, but suddenly our doxologies of gratitude for being the most blessed nation on earth seem to have been replaced by slogans meant to bolster our fading spirit.

Do not think that I am predicting a sudden collapse of America (although I must regretfully say that I would not be shocked to wake up some day to its sudden demise). The industrial machines of America probably will keep on running. Its fluorescent lights probably will go on burning. The kaleidoscope cornucopia called

Western capitalism probably will keep rolling out its consumer goodies.

What I fear is a growing sense of entropy. I have an anxiety that stems from a feeling that this nation, which I love, appears no longer to have any good reason to go on living. I have the sense that our country no longer has a dream or a vision that it seeks to realize.

Something sad appears to have happened to America. Perhaps because we have gained everything materially worth having, now our only raison d'être is to figure out how to hold onto it. Perhaps we have become a people who are frightened of having our hard-earned gains slip away from us. It is difficult to figure out just what the problem is. But I do know that there is a problem. As a people we have become nervous and uncertain of ourselves. There is evidence that we have become afraid of our future.

CHAPTER 2

IS THERE A PROPHET IN THE HOUSE?

WHEN THE NEW PREACHER came to town, everybody at the Baptist church was talking about how good he was and how much better he was than their old preacher. The town skeptic inquired with great interest of one of the deacons what this new man was preaching that made him so different from the old preacher.

"The old preacher told us we were all lost sinners and unless we repented we were all going to hell," was the answer.

"Well, what does this new preacher say?" the skeptic asked.

"This new preacher tells us we are all lost sinners and unless we repent we are all going to hell," was the reply.

"Well I'll be damned if I can tell the difference," was the skeptic's judgment.

"Oh there's a big difference," answered the deacon.

"This one says it with tears in his eyes."

That, of course, is the mark of the true prophet. The true prophet makes his judgments and pronounces his warnings with tears in his eyes. Like Jeremiah, he weeps.

> Is there no balm in Gilead; is there no physician there? why then is not the health of the daughter of my people recovered? (Jer. 8:22)

He knows that history will take its course and that, unless there is a real repentance, the people he loves and the nation to which he belongs will be no more. He grieves, "O earth, earth, earth..." (Jer. 22:29) because he knows that his people are dying and there is no future for the present order. With the true prophet there is weeping and gnashing of teeth.

We need a prophet like that in America today. We need more than a sociological critique explaining what is wrong with us and how we got this way. We need a prophet who will weep for America, who will stir us to a memory of what we were meant to be, who will reach into our collective consciousness and who will draw out of it the sorrowful memory of the real American dream.

Such a prophet will not only weep floods of tears for America but also teach all of us to weep. And in that weeping lies our only hope, because it is the weeping that can break the numbness of our hearts and minds. It is the grieving that can teach us how to feel again. It is that weeping taught to us by the prophet that can break the mesmerizing spell of the deadly present and can show us how to be passionate again.

The Prophet As Dreamer

But weeping is only half of what the prophet will have to do. There is an even greater responsibility to be carried out. The task of the prophet is to nurture, nourish, and evoke a vision of an alternative to the dominant system. The prophet must generate hope for something that lies beyond the present order. We need a vision of an alternative future that will energize us and motivate us to act, a vision of possibilities that will make our blood run hot and give us the courage to revolt against the way things are.

A prophet's vision can replace people's numbness with energy. The possibility of a glorious "might be" can enable us to live in ways that appear dangerous to the custodians of the status quo. With vision, the dead bones can come alive. The psychically dead can be resurrected. The spiritual sleepers can be awakened. Out of sorrow for the death of the old can come a new dynamism to us; through the message of the prophet we can come to believe in a new heaven and a new earth. The apathy that works in people in dying societies can be dispelled. There can be passion. There can be a "new song" (Isa. 42:10), and the fatigue that is so evident among those in the present order can be overcome:

> Hast thou not known? hast thou not heard, that the everlasting God, the LORD, the Creator of the ends of the earth, fainteth not, neither is weary? there is no searching of his understanding.

He giveth power to the faint; and to them that
have no might he increaseth strength.
Even the youths shall faint and be weary, and
the young men shall utterly fall:
But they that wait upon the LORD shall renew
their strength; they shall mount up with wings
as eagles: they shall run, and not be weary; and
they shall walk, and not faint. (Isaiah 40:28–31)

All of this energy comes from the message of the
prophet. The people of the dying society can be "born
again." The prophet's hope can generate the dynamism
for change.

A Need for a Prophet in the Last Days

America needs more than a patch-up job. Its sin goes
deeper that anything that can be remedied with some
improvements here and there. That is why the would-be
prophets who preach at our religious convocations fail to
measure up. Their messages may point out major flaws
in our system and even call us to repentance, but something more is needed, something more profound and far-
reaching. We need a voice crying in the wilderness of our
consumer-oriented cultural system that will prepare the
way of the Lord.

Who Might the Prophet Be?

Not too long ago I sat with some young people and
reflected on the times in which we live. In the course of
our discussions, I brought up America's need for a
prophet. I asked these young people to tell me what such
a prophet might be like if God should raise one up today.

I wanted to know which voice out of the historical past they thought that America most needed to hear today. One suggestion was Martin Luther King. And I could see some justification for that suggestion.

For a little while, King's voice called us away from the deadness of our consumer-oriented way of life and challenged us to an idealism of an America that is "not yet." What he said and how he said it almost shook us from our drowsiness. He almost made us believe that we had a higher calling and a more noble destiny than we were living out. We resonated to his words as he set forth his prophetic vision:

> I say to you today, my friends, that in spite of the difficulties and frustrations of the moment I still have a dream. It is a dream deeply rooted in the American dream.
>
> I have a dream that one day this nation will rise up and live out the true meaning of its creed: "We hold these truths to be self-evident; that all men are created equal."
>
> I have a dream that one day on the red hills of Georgia the sons of former slaves and the sons of former slaveowners will be able to sit down together at the table of brotherhood.
>
> I have a dream that one day even the state of Mississippi, a desert state sweltering with the heat of injustice and oppression, will be transformed into an oasis of freedom and justice.
>
> I have a dream that my four little children will one day live in a nation where they will not be judged by the color of their skin but by the content of their character.

I have a dream today.

I have a dream that one day the state of Alabama, whose governor's lips are presently dripping with words of interposition and nullification, will be transformed into a situation where little black boys and black girls will be able to join hands with little white boys and white girls and walk together as sisters and brothers.

I have a dream today.

I have a dream that one day every valley shall be exalted, every hill and mountain shall be made low, the rough places will be made plain, and the crooked places will be made straight, and the glory of the Lord shall be revealed, and all flesh shall see it together.

Another commonly mentioned name was Mahatma Gandhi. Fresh from seeing the motion picture about his life, these young people were stirred by the ways in which this man, living out the Sermon on the Mount, had profoundly altered the course of history for India and England.

I had to agree that Gandhi's heroic call to nonviolent opposition to tyranny, his compassionate plea for people to recognize their common sacred humanity, and his hope for a world in which spiritual sensitivity to all living creatures might prevail all amounted to a message for our time.

As our discussion continued there was one, above all others, who all of these bright and idealistic young people agreed had the traits of a prophet and the message that America most needed to hear. This was St. Francis of Assisi.

St. Francis of Assisi

The suggestion that St. Francis could be a prophet for our time took me by surprise. It seemed strange that a medieval saint of the Roman Catholic church should be the voice that a group of Protestant young people thought would be most relevant to our time. But these young people knew more about St. Francis than I had imagined, and their case for him being the saint for our times proved increasingly convincing. There is something intriguingly attractive about this pre-Renaissance man who called himself "a clown for God." There is a mystical quality about his character that has a magnetizing effect on people like us.

St. Francis for Today

I am sure that if St. Francis were with us today, he would not so much condemn us for our consumer-oriented materialism as he would weep over our failure to see where life and love can be most fully experienced and actualized—among the poor. He would not so much tell us that having things is bad as he would tell us that giving what we have to the poor can enliven us to God and to the highest potentialities of our humanity.

For Francis, being Christian was, above all else, being committed to and in love with the poor. Like many of the modern Liberation Theologians, Francis found in the poor a special presence of God, and he made loving the poor synonymous with loving Christ. He said: I love the poor, not because they are poor but because Jesus is in them. Whenever I embrace them I embrace Our Lord.

To Francis, the poor were sacramental. He found infused in their personhood the real presence of Christ. He was convinced that as he embraced the poor he embraced the Lord Himself. Jesus is there not only symbolically; according to Francis, He is *really* there. It made no difference to him whether the poor were holy or Christian. Even among the most despicable of them, Francis contended that he could experience Christ's real presence. To him, Matthew 25:40 was to be taken literally.

Undoubtedly, the disposition of Francis to the poor was grounded in his own personal experience. According to his own report, his understanding of who is in the poor was revealed to him through a dramatic event in his own life.

While Francis was traveling by horseback down a lonely road, a begging leper dressed in rags suddenly blocked his way. Lepers had always been a repulsive sight to Francis. He became nauseated just being near them. And there before him was a leper who could not be avoided.

At that moment Francis heard the words of Jesus resounding in his heart: "As you do it to the least of these, my brothers, you do it to me!"

Francis climbed off his horse and went up to the leper. He not only gave him all of his money but also gave him his clothes. Then, on impulse, he embraced the leper and kissed him.

Climbing back onto his horse, Francis glanced down toward where the leper had been to bid him farewell. Shocked, he realized that the road was empty. The leper had vanished. All that Francis could conclude was that he who he thought had been a leper had really been the Lord Himself. What he had done for that leper, Francis was convinced, he had done for Christ.

In light of that experience, it is easy to understand why Francis would consider every poor person a kind of incarnation of the resurrected Lord, waiting to be loved and served. It is also easy to understand why Mother Teresa, a twentieth-century counterpart of St. Francis, should say that whenever she looks into the eyes of the poor she literally sees Jesus looking back at her. Nor is it any wonder that this group of young Christians should find in Francis the model for their lives and a prophet for our times.

We do not need some wild-eyed pulpiteer condemning us for our consumer-oriented ways as much as we need such a wet-eyed saint, pleading with us to find fulfillment and ecstasy in service to the poor. We need this kind of pleading voice urging us to find the Eternal in the faces of the oppressed.

The Franciscan Commitment to Peace

St. Francis also was committed to peace, which makes him attractive to my young friends. Their generation has become cynical about wars, and they are not about to be hoodwinked by the slogans of politicians. They know that economic interests lie behind the propaganda about saving people from totalitarianism. Whether it be in El Salvador or in the Middle East, the real reason for U.S. intervention is to hold on to the resources that keep our consumer-oriented society going. And these young people have had enough. They long for a voice that will put

the sacredness of human life above the values of the
affluent way of life. They find that voice in St. Francis.

With Francis, peace was not just an absence of war created by a balance of power. Instead, it was an attitude
toward those who would define themselves as enemies.
Francis would have no part of the Crusades, which in his
day were obligatory service for those who would be
devout Christians. He could not look on the Muslims as
persons to be hated and slain any more than he could
look that way on his Lord. He had only one goal as far as
the followers of Islam were concerned, and that was to
tell them about Jesus and help them to realize that in
Jesus they could all be brothers and sisters.

With some of the members of his order Francis went
out one day to meet those so-called enemies of the cross.
He did not go with a sword or a bow; he went armed
only with love and grace. He must have seemed like a
crazy man to those worshipers of Allah who knew how
to do only one thing to the Christians who challenged
them. Yet there must have been a mystical presence
about that son-of-merchant-turned-saint. There must
have been something awesome about that strange man
dressed in burlap with a piece of rough rope tied around
his waist.

Surprisingly, the enemy army received him as an hon-
ored guest and gave him an audience with their sultan.
Nobody knows what Francis said and did in the sultan's
tent. It may have been that Francis talked theology and
did a bit of Christian apologetics. But I think not. I have
a sense that this simple monk did nothing more and
nothing less than love the sultan and share with him the
source of that love, who is Christ Jesus.

There is no indication that the sultan was converted, and there is every indication that Francis was disappointed. He would be neither the first nor the last prophet of God who would have his love rejected. But he tried. And to this day, he symbolizes for all of us the radical attitude toward one's enemies prescribed by Jesus. It is an attitude set forth in the Sermon on the Mount. It is an attitude seldom lived out in a world where people trust more in power than in love, and where "realism" dictates that you do in your enemy before your enemy does you in.

The early church was pacifist, but they would turn from that pacifist posture once Constantine made Christianity the religion of the empire. After all, the pragmatists argue, you owe a favor or two to an emperor who gives your religion such prestige. That's how the system works. And so Christendom blessed the Empire and sanctified its armies. The priests, who were placed in the royal court, dictated that Constantine's wars were "holy" wars, and the cross replaced the eagle on the Roman standard.

It would be centuries before St. Francis of Assisi would recover Christ's message about what to do about one's enemies. But the pacifist mindset, derived from a literal reading of the Sermon on the Mount, is gaining an ever-widening acceptance among present-day young people and among some older ones too. More and more Christians are becoming convinced that the New Testament does not allow for killing, even in battle, and they look for a prophet who will tell this to the church.

Certainly, the Vietnam War has had a great deal to do with the pacifist inclinations of these young people, but

there is a deeper reason why the Franciscan understanding of violence is increasingly taking hold of them. I
think it is because it is a belief whose time has come. It
is as though it is a truth that has come of age, a doctrine
with an affinity for our people, a message that we, more
and more, are ready to hear. What Jesus showed us about
loving our enemies and how St. Francis believed and
practiced it seems relevant and even obvious to a new
breed of Christians.

When they see what is happening because of the eye-
for-an-eye and tooth-for-a-tooth way of life in the ghettos, the senselessness of violence becomes more and
more clear. They see the futility of killing as a way of
resolving anything. And as they live and work in a culture that is permeated with retributive concepts of justice, they only hope to establish what Jesus called "a
more excellent way."

St. Francis's Respect for Nature

No prophetic judgment on contemporary America
would be adequate without addressing the ecological disaster perpetrated because of our consumeristic ways.
Our disregard for nature has resulted in the extinction of
large numbers of both animal and plant species. What
we have done to both the oceans and the atmosphere has
raised serious doubts about the survival of life here on
spaceship earth. In such a context, it is easy to see that
for these young Christians what Francis taught about
being related to our physical and biological environ-
ments takes on a quality of urgency.

The respect and love that Francis had for animals are
legendary. While some of the tales told about this gentle

monk might indeed be apocryphal, they must be at least based on truth. Whether or not he was in such empathy with nature that he was able to talk to birds is something that is impossible to prove. Nevertheless, most people are familiar with the claim and have seen pictures and statues depicting that claim. That he had a mystical relationship with animals is undoubtedly true.

There is nothing "New Age" about such claims. After all, Jesus was able to do the same. When our Lord spoke, even the winds and the waves obeyed Him. Why couldn't the man who many claim most nearly imitated Christ have done a little of the same?

According to one of the most famous stories about Francis, he was able to make a "brother" out of an animal. It seems that there was a wolf who regularly attacked the herds of sheep owned by the farmers of Assisi. So many sheep were being killed that the doings of that wolf proved to be a threat to the economic well-being of the town. The shepherds felt that the menace posed by the wolf could no longer be ignored, and they gathered themselves together and decided to track him down collectively and destroy him. When Francis heard what the shepherds had planned, he intervened with a proposal. What Francis asked was for permission to go into the hills and seek out the wolf and personally deal with the creature. Only if he failed, he told them, would they then be free to hunt the wolf and kill him. The farmers agreed with Francis's plan and gave him a few days to carry it out.

When Francis returned to Assisi a few days later, the one-time terrible wolf was following along behind him like some kind of pet puppy dog. Francis had tamed the

wolf with love and kindness. He had turned the beast
into a friend. He had participated in a limited way with
the redemption of the fallen nature.

The creatures of nature, as demonstrated by Francis,
have the potential to be in sacred communion with us
and even to be transformed through our love for them.
We, as humans, can be like older brothers and sisters to
animals. We can sense, according to Francis, a limited
but, nevertheless, real kinship not only with animals but
with the entire physical universe.

If we are to take Francis at his word, the stars and the
planets are not to be taken as the "dead" assemblages of
molecules that the physicists have told us that they are.
According to Francis, we can pray for our "brother the
wolf" and talk in an almost intimate way about the sun
and the moon. Without hesitancy he asks of birds:

> My brother birds, you ought always to praise
> and love your Creator who has given you feath-
> ers for clothing, wings for flight, and all that
> you have need of. He has given you a dwelling
> in the purity of the air, though you sow not,
> neither do you reap.

and also:

> Praised be my Lord God with all his creatures
> and especially our brother the sun, who brings
> us the day and who brings us the light; fair is he
> and shines with a very great splendor: O Lord,
> he signifies to us Thee.
>
> Praised be my Lord for our sister the moon,
> and for the stars, the which he hath set clear
> and lovely in the heavens.

This is no sentimental pantheism (although mystics are often accused of being pantheists). Nor is it some kind of Spinozan monism (although he, like Spinoza, acknowledges some kind of spiritual solidarity with nature). It is simply part of the prayerful attitude of one who loves his Lord and is conscious that in everything that exists, God is at work keeping it together and giving it vitality.

> For by him were all things created, that are in heaven, and that are in earth, visible and invisible, whether they be thrones, or dominions, or principalities, or powers: all things were created by him, and for him:
> And he is before all things, and by him all things consist. (Col. 1:16–17)

Such an attitude toward nature is essential for us to learn if we are to survive in this world and have some kind of harmonious relationship with nature. We must move beyond a theology of domination of the geosphere and biosphere that allows for the exploitation of nature, and we must develop a belief system that places us in joyful empathy with nature. On course we must avoid the kind of fuzzy anthropomorphic religiosity of animism and the kind of religio-magic occultism that mark the New Age movement. Somehow we must reestablish that respectful awe of nature that was so brilliantly modeled for us in St. Francis. In some way we must learn how to revere the animals, the plants, and even the inanimate realms of nature. And we must do it without attributing more in the way of spiritual essence to nature than the Bible allows.

If we learn what St. Francis can teach us, we will no longer kill the animals for sport or pollute the water and the air as we produce the things we think we need. We will no longer be aliens in a strange and distant land. Instead, we will be at home in a world that is ablaze with signs of holiness. We will find our rightful place in the wonder of it all.

St. Francis, to my young friends, is more and more being defined as the saint for the next decade. His spirituality is a model for those who would repent of the havoc wreaked on nature. We have in St. Francis a glimpse of what we all should be if we are to survive into the twenty-first century.

St. Francis's Familiarity with the Miraculous

There is one last thing that made St. Francis the ideal prophet for these young Christians, who, in some ways, may embody the longings of a whole new church. It was his devotional life. In his prayer life he experienced such a oneness with Christ that he, like some say was true of the Apostle Paul, bore the marks of the Lord's crucifixion. Those who study the life of St. Francis cannot escape the story of his wilderness experience on the mountain during which he came to bear in his body the stigmata of Christ.

An aristocrat from Tuscany named Orlando of Chiusi, upon meeting Francis, wanted to give him a gift as an act of courtesy. The gift turned out to be a strange one. It was a mountain. Not prone to accepting any gifts that would make him other than a poor man, it was surprising that Francis should accept this gift. But he did.

The mountain became a place where Francis would go for prayer and fasting. When he went there, he did not take even his closest friend, Alverno of Apennines. Thus, no one was present when "the miracle" happened. Nor is anyone sure of the date and time of the miracle. The scholars still debate such details. *What* really happened is also questionable, since Francis spoke of it to only one other person.

The most anyone knows is that while on the mountain Francis had a vision. In it he saw in the heavens a vast winged figure that was either crucified or in the posture of a crucifixion. The vision was of colossal proportions. The whole heaven was filled with some vast immemorial power. It was like some gigantic wounded bird. The cries of pain that came from the winged revelation pierced the soul of Francis with sorrow and compassion. When the vision faded from the sky a vast silence filled the morning, and Francis came down from the mountain with the nail prints of Christ's crucifixion in his own hands.

In America an emerging new breed of Christians strongly identifies with this kind of mysticism and with this kind of encounter with the transcendental. These people are tired of the commercialized kinds of displays of so-called miracles that are accessible by a mere flip of the TV dial. They are left unsatisfied with the sterile rationalism of much theology.

When Moses came down from Sinai, his face was so radiant with the glory of God that a veil was needed to keep the children of Israel from being blinded by him. When Jacob came down from the mountain, he was so possessed by a blessing from his wrestling with "the angel of the Lord" that he was a new person. When St. Francis came down from his mountain, his hands and feet bore the nail prints of His Savior, and in his side there was a wound similar to that made by a Roman soldier who once thrust a spear into the body of the Son of Man. In Francis there was an answer to the prayer prayed by Paul:

> That I may know him, and the power of his resurrection, and the fellowship of his sufferings, being made comfortable unto his death. (Phil. 3:10)

It is not the kind of experience that some more "rational" thinkers might call "religio-magic" that was of prime concern to the young people who talked with me about Francis. Instead, it is the closeness with Christ that this story points to that was the focus of their longings. They seemed tired of theologies that have all the answers and churches that "program" them to death. These young people wanted to *experience* God. They wanted to *feel* God tingling in their hearts. They wanted some Dionysian ecstasy in the spirit. And they wanted a prophet who would condemn any church that offered them less. They wanted to be alive in Christ and to have Christ alive in them. They were not asking for a sign in the sky, or a sudden rending of the natural order of things. They were asking for a prophet who would declare that there was still the possibility for the miracle that could take away the deadness of their souls.

Francis showed them how to experience that miracle. It would come in the midst of long hours of prayer. It would come in the midst of struggling and suffering in the dark. It would come in the midst of earnestly and endlessly pleading with God to explode within them. Ironically, it would come in the midst of these spiritual disciplines, but not because of them. Francis made them know that the miracle they sought comes as a *gift*. But he taught them how to "wait upon the Lord" in order to be ready for that gift. Francis made them believe that the gift could be theirs. And that is why they would make him a prophet for our times.

CHAPTER 3

AN ETHIC FOR CHRISTIANS AND OTHER ALIENS IN A STRANGE AND DISTANT LAND

GETTING INVOLVED WITH
the poor can convert people, and it usually does. Sometimes the conversions come while walking the streets of a Hispanic barrio. Sometimes they come while trying to tutor educationally disadvantaged kids in some low-cost government housing community. But however they come, among those who become directly and emotionally involved with people whom the world has rejected, conversions seem inevitable.

This special conversion, which belongs primarily to those who accept the challenge that the original rich young ruler refused (Mark 10:17-22), brings with it new revelations and truths. They are revelations that can tell people what a prophet might tell them if they could meet one face to face. They are revelations about America and about themselves that people would rather not have because they tell them of the shallowness of their discipleship and the phoniness of their spirituality. There is the discovery that is often made when people work among the poor about the failure of the church to be the church that Christ wanted it to be. In all of these revelations there is something that usually breaks through and forges a new state of consciousness.

This conversion at the hands of the poor makes people weep and shout angrily at their priests and preachers:

> Why didn't you tell us? Why did you hide the truth from us? You knew that the real Jesus bids us come and die. Yet you told us that if we believed right and lived decent lives we'd be okay. You knew the cost of discipleship was high. Yet you told us that all that would be required of us would be to live up to religious respectability. Why did you have us ignore the radical commandments of the Bible and why did you blind us with an easy belief that concealed the truth?

A New Breed of Christians

There are an increasing number who have gone through such spiritual trauma and have come out as a new breed of Christians. These new Christians are easily identifiable, although they do not as yet have a name. The founders of *Sojourners* magazine once called them "post-American Christians." Some Mennonite writers refer to them as "Radical Reformation Christians." So far, no particular label has stuck. But they are out there across America, and they are growing in number.

One of the marks of this "second" conversion is a turning away from the consumeristic life-style of the American middle class. Those who have had it opt for a more responsible use of money. There is among them a profound repentance for having so many things that they do not need when there are many who do not have what is essential to survive.

This new breed of Christians raises questions about what kind of cars they have a right to drive. They give careful consideration to the kind of clothes they have a right to buy and to the kind of places where they ought to live.

Case Study I

In the Pacific Northwest, several Christian couples have pooled their resources and talents to build their own houses. Instead of having to pay close to a million dollars in interest, as does the typical middle-class home buyer who has a long-term mortgage, they are building homes that can be had at the cost of building materials and land. With such huge savings to each young married couple there is going to be a great deal of money available to "do ministry" for people in need.

These houses are by no means ugly, squeezed-in boxes. They are designed to be beautiful. There will be colors and there will be charm. These houses will be works of art. One of the intentions of these young married couples is to show that an alternative life-style can be beautiful. They are out to dispel the myth that a fortune has to be spent to have what is attractive and joyful. Paintings that they themselves have created will decorate their walls and hand crafts will liven up their shelves and ledges. They are out to show that to be in the image of God who makes things beautiful requires that we make things beautiful, too. They are out to prove that the simple life-style need not be ugly.

Case Study II

There is a group of about two hundred people living together in a Christian community in Chicago. They call themselves the Jesus People USA. Among their many ventures are the publication of a cutting-edge magazine and the sponsoring of one of America's foremost Christian rock groups, *Rez Band*. Jesus People USA takes in all kinds of people, particularly street people who otherwise would have no home. The group has initiated a number of small businesses, including a roofing business and a cleaning business. A number of its people are into rehabilitating houses for the poor. All the money that is earned from these ventures is put into a common pot, and, as in the early church, individuals get what they require in accordance with their respective needs.

Visiting the Jesus People USA is, in some respects, a return to the counterculture life-styles of the sixties. Their hair, their dress, and their manner give the impression that they are a baptized version of the flower people. But everyone who visits comes away with a sense that they have encountered authentic Christianity. The Jesus People USA are a wonder to behold.

Case Study III

In Pittsburgh, Pennsylvania, there are some young doctors fresh out of medical school who have modeled a sacrificial life-style in a profession that has been far too seduced by the allurements of big money. They have established a clinic that is housed in the basement of a church, and they are offering medical services on the basis of people's ability to pay. There are poor people who get the best kind of treatment available in today's world for little or no money.

It should be noted that there are many well-off people who go to these doctors too, but they are expected to pay what is typical for good medical care. As a matter of fact, there are many pastors in middle-class churches throughout the Pittsburgh area who encourage their people to go to this clinic, because the money paid by those who can afford to pay is what keeps the clinic going.

These young doctors could be on their way to becoming millionaires. Instead, they earn a very modest living. They have rejected the ways of the world and have become radical followers of another Great Physician. They are part of this emerging new breed of Christians who owe more of their understanding of Christianity to Dietrich Bonhoeffer than to the teachings of mainline churches. They are the fruits of a prophetic mentality that seems to be picking up momentum daily.

A Theology for the New Breed

A theology is being worked out by these radical Christians as they carry out their grassroots efforts among the poor. It is not some new formulation of doctrine. Actually, this new breed of countercultural Christians is holding to what some might call "the old-time religion."

They are strikingly evangelical and, for the most part, believe in the historical creeds of the church. They take the Bible as an infallible message from God, although they remain aloof from the debate over inerrancy that seems to preoccupy most Fundamentalists. When pressed, they are likely to admit to some problems with the biblical text, particularly with those passages that seem to prohibit women from roles of leadership. But they seem generally unimpressed with those erudite arguments that come from "lower" and "higher" textual criticism. Like Mark Twain, they are not bothered by the things about the Bible that they don't understand; it's the things that they do understand that bother them. What Jesus says in the Sermon on the Mount and what He says in the twenty-fifth chapter of Matthew is the focus of their attention.

If anything makes these people unique, it is the emphasis they put on the Gospel writers. Christians, particularly Protestant Christians, usually have learned to understand Jesus through the eyes of the Apostle Paul. Early in their spiritual development most Protestants pick up the categories of Pauline theology and then filter what they read in the Gospels through that grid. There is nothing wrong with this, but it does make for an emphasis in interpreting scripture other than would be gained by reading the Pauline epistles from an orientation established by first reading the Gospels. If one's basic understanding of what it means to be Christian comes from Pauline teachings, then what is primary about being a Christian is *believing* the right things. Thus, the doctrines about substitutionary atonement, eternal security, predestination, and the second coming of Christ are of paramount importance.

These were the concerns I had while I was young. In the summer Bible conferences I attended, some Bible teacher usually took us through one of Paul's epistles. Bible study groups I joined always seemed to make Pauline theology the focus of attention. In fact, I cannot remember ever systematically studying the Gospels during the entire time I was growing up. Once again, I must affirm that there is nothing wrong with this. It is just that it is easy when using this approach to become so preoccupied with what it is we are supposed to *believe* that we can lose sight of what we as Christians are supposed to *do*.

It is the Gospels that clarify in detail the radical nature and cost of discipleship. It is the Gospels that make us aware that obedience to Christ's commandments is at the core of what it means to love Christ and to be part of His Kingdom. If you think about it, you will realize that it really does make a difference if you read the Gospels through the perspective provided by the Epistles or if you read the Epistles through the perspective provided by the Gospels. The difference is not a matter of truth but a matter of emphasis. The Epistles emphasize doctrine and the Gospels emphasize life-style.

This new breed of radical Christians tends to take the Gospels quite literally. These people make obedience to the life-style prescribed by Christ their primary objective. While believing in all the Pauline doctrines that are so dear to those of us who claim to hold to orthodox theologies, their primary concerns seem to be focused on how, out of gratitude to God for His grace, they can be faithful imitators of His Son.

Recognizing this emphasis on the life-style prescribed by Christ, it is not surprising that these radical counterculture Christians should derive much of their inspiration from the heroes and heroines of Roman Catholicism. They are more prone to read what Thomas à Kempis wrote than what Calvin wrote. They are more likely to be awed by Mother Teresa than by famous Protestant preachers. And they are more inclined to believe that St. Francis got to the heart of what the Gospel is about than they are inclined to be impressed with the writings of Martin Luther.

Some Warnings to These "New" Christians

While there is much to admire in the new counterculture Christians who seem to be popping up from coast to coast, there is also something a bit frightening about them. They often give the rest of us a sense that they have espoused a new legalism. Those in the old Fundamentalist subculture made giving up dancing, movies, and booze the evidence of being *really* born again. Now these new "simple life-style" Christians tend to come across as suggesting that only those who are radically committed to being antiestablishment have any hope of being part of the Kingdom of God.

Both to the earlier Fundamentalists and to those who promote a radical commitment to the literal message laid down in the Sermon on the Mount there comes the declaration that we are saved by *grace* and not by *works* (Eph. 2:8–9). That means that Jesus did what was necessary to make us acceptable to God and that we do not have to do a lot of good things to earn His favor. While radically embracing a Franciscan way of life at the tail end of the twentieth century may be a good form of rebellion against the spiritually stifling effects of a consumer-oriented society, it does not make us into people worthy of going to heaven. While giving up the things that our culture has conditioned us to crave and experiencing God's presence in ministry to the poor may be the most "reasonable service" (Rom. 12:1) to offer to Him, such things do not determine His love for us. The good news is that He loves us anyway and nothing can change that.

A moving expression of grace was provided by the parents of a graduate of the college where I teach when their son, a young Korean man, was brutally and senselessly murdered on the streets of Philadelphia. In Ho Ho had graduated with honors from Eastern College and was in the process of completing graduate studies in medicine at the University of Pennsylvania when he was killed. While mailing a letter to his family in Korea, he was surrounded by a gang of teenage hoods, robbed of the change in his pockets, and beaten to death.

Even though there are murders daily in the City of Brotherly Love, the ugliness and callous nature of this murder sent shock waves through the city. The police went all out to find the culprits and within three days had them behind bars.

The murderers proved to be a sorry lot. They were homeless boys who had grown up on the streets, "throwaway" kids not wanted by anyone. They were illiterate and unskilled and had learned to survive in their cold and violent ghetto by becoming cold and violent themselves.

When the trial of these murderers was held, In Ho Ho's parents flew to America to be in attendance. They sat motionless all during the legal proceedings. They said nothing at all during the trial. They only asked for an opportunity to speak after the "guilty" verdict was announced. It was then that they stepped forward and kneeled in front of the judge's bench.

Before a stunned audience, these parents begged for mercy for their son's murderers. Not only were they devoid of any "eye for an eye and tooth for a tooth" mentality, but they wanted to help these despicable young men.

They begged the judge to release their son's murderers to them so that they could give the boys the home and care they had never had. They were Christians, they explained to the judge, and they wanted to show something of the grace they had received from God to those who had done them such grievous evil.

The judge, who newspaper reporters claimed had a reputation for being hard and unemotional, had tears in his eyes as he explained, "That is not the way our system of justice works."

Indeed, it is not!

The good news about the grace of God is that it isn't earned by goodness and it is handed out to those who are completely undeserving. That, of course, is why I am sure that it applies to me. No intense commitment to literally living out the Sermon on the Mount and no embracing of a Christian countercultural life-style can earn God's love. It is a free gift waiting to be accepted.

A Recognition of Middle-Range Christians

Another thing that worries me about those whose embracing of the prophetic message leads them to break completely with the ways of our consumer-oriented society is their lack of patience with any of us who do not go "all the way" with them. Too often I have felt like a third-class Christian around these people because I have a house in suburbia and drive a half-decent car. Those who live in condos, have "establishment-type" jobs, and on occasion go to Hawaii for vacations sometimes are made to feel that they have no right to claim to be followers of Jesus. What the countercultural Christians fail to realize is that there are a lot of us who have sensed the call of the prophetic message and are aware of the spiritual bankruptcy of our culture who may not be ready or able to abandon completely a lot of the things that go with the "good life American style." They do not seem to realize that in addition to those who drop everything to follow Jesus, there are some of us who do not go the whole nine yards, but who still make *some* changes and do *some* things that are signs of the Kingdom.

There are some of us who are what I will call *middle-range Christians*. We believe in the message of the prophet but are still a part of "the system." We relate to those who call us to a simple life-style, but we still have kids to raise and we want to raise them middle class and send them to college. We still have bills to pay. We may even be married to people who don't understand our vision. We know all of those biblical admonitions about going halfway and being lukewarm, and we confess an uneasiness about them. But we still contend that *something is better than nothing*. We still believe that there is something we can do to change America even if we fall far short of the likes of Mother Teresa. We will not throw up our hands and give up, just because we cannot do all that we know we are supposed to do if we are to be a Kingdom people.

We believe that we middle-range Christians can carry out middle-range projects that will do a lot of good. What we give after office hours may not seem like much to the radically committed, but we believe that we make a difference. While we still spend a lot of money for things that we don't need, we nevertheless find some joy in sending a monthly gift to support a Third World child with World Vision or in supporting a hospice for people with AIDS. So give us a break!

In the days of the early church there were many who sold all that they had and made their resources available for the work of God. Barnabas may have been the best of them. Special note is made of him in the fourth chapter of Acts.

There must have been tremendous pressure in the early church to measure up to the standard set by Barnabas. Apparently such pressure was felt by two of those church members named Annias and Sapphira. These two, it seems, wanting to appear as committed as Barnabas, lived a lie. They pretended to have given all, but they secretly held some of their wealth in reserve.

Peter's response to the action of Annias and Sapphira was severe judgment. Both of them were struck dead (Acts 5:1–11). But Peter makes the point that it was not the holding back of money that was their sin, but the *pretense* of having given all. Concealing the truth that they were still holding on to some of their worldly possessions while grandstanding as having given all was the "lie against the Holy Spirit."

To be like Barnabas is ideal. However, many of us hold back some of what we have and cling to some of the things that we have been culturally conditioned to want. We do not rationalize our possessions and life-style, looking for proof texts to make our case. We do not justify our actions with some convoluted theology. But we will not lie. We will tell you that we still are into our consumer-oriented life-style. And we will also tell you that we are making strides toward change. We are not what we should be, but we are not what we were.

If you are one of us, take hope. We are doing something to break the hold on our consciousness that the world once held. The limited things that we accomplish mean *something* in the grand scheme of things. Remember, we are saved by a King who promises that even a glass of water given in his name will have its reward (Matthew 10:42). We are the middle-range Christians.

CHAPTER 4

THE "BOTTOMS UP" REVOLUTION

SOME YEARS AGO, I TOOK A
group of my students from Eastern College on a study
tour of the Dominican Republic. While there, we visited
a barrio in the capital city, Santo Domingo. I wanted my
students to experience firsthand the influence of the
charismatic movement that had been sweeping across
Latin America.

I had come to know a Roman Catholic priest in this
particular barrio whose ministry had been dramatically
transformed as the result of a Pentecostal experience.
This priest was into speaking in tongues and carrying
out faith healings. His Sunday morning congregation
had grown from a mere handful to several hundred worshipers.

There were reports of spiritual revival throughout this
slum area. There were large numbers of personal conversions and changed family life. The people who had

opened themselves up to this new kind of spirituality were dramatically altering their life-styles. Prostitutes were giving up "the life" and settling down to being respectable mothers. Men were marrying the women who had borne their children and were becoming responsible fathers. A school had been started. A clinic had been established. A literacy program had been put into place.

I wanted my students to take a look at this Pentecostal revival in process and to explore how personal conversions work themselves out in social change. I had planned for them to begin their encounter with this priest and his ministries. I wanted them to experience the spiritual dynamism that could be generated by a simple Sunday morning Mass. None of us was prepared for what we were about to see and hear.

We arrived at the church about a half hour before the service was supposed to start. The cinder-block building with its tin roof was already filled, and we were glad to find some standing room in the back. During the half hour that followed at least a couple hundred people showed up too late to get in and had to stand outside and listen to the service via a public address system.

The tropical temperature was already more than we North Americans were used to, and the body heat generated by the press of bodies in these squeezed quarters made conditions almost unbearable. What was immediately noticeable was that there did not seem to be any of the jovial spirit that I had come to expect from such Pentecostal gatherings. Instead, there was a sense of solemn concern among the people. There was an air of serious anticipation as the congregation waited for the service to begin.

My students and I were soon to learn that the people of this barrio were facing a painful future. In order to develop the tourist trade, the government had decided to tear down their barrio. It was located on the bank of the only river that flowed through the city, and government officials had decided that it was the ideal place to construct a marina to serve the tourist trade. The idea that these people, who were squatters with no legal rights to the land on which their shacks had been built, were to be displaced in order to create a playground for rich people with yachts, came across to us as the worst kind of economic oppression.

Each week the priest, along with a group of representatives from the barrio, would go to the government offices and plead for some relief from the impending disaster. Then on Sundays, during Mass, the priest would report on how the negotiations had gone. The people listened in rapt attention as the priest told them what had happened during the discussions at the presidential palace. The intensity of the listening gave obvious evidence of the urgency of the situation. The discussions were about these people's survival.

When the priest had finished his report, he allowed for questions from the congregation. One young man seated on the front row of the church rose and asked, "But, Father, what if all of these talks fail? What if all you try to do comes to nothing and they come with bulldozers to destroy our homes? What will we do then, Father? What will we do then?"

But before the priest could answer, another voice took control of the crowd. A young man standing close to us in the rear of that overcrowded church shouted out,

"Then I will fight them! If they come to destroy our homes, I will fight them!"

Then, in a move that had overtones of demagoguery, he shouted at the crowd, "Are you with me? Are you with me?"

Without hesitation, the people shouted back at him, "We are with you! We are with you! We are with you!" The applause and cheering that followed was deafening.

In the midst of this turmoil the priest screamed out, "Silence! Silence!" And as the crowd fell still, he reached for the eucharist, held up the cup and declared, "In this coming struggle, Jesus is with you, too!"

Welcome to Liberation Theology

Later in the afternoon, my students got together with me. Visibly shaken by what had transpired at the morning Mass, they wanted to talk about what it all meant. Convinced that a violent confrontation was inevitable, it seemed to them that there were only three ways of looking at the situation:

1. Jesus is not involved in such political situations. If this is the case, then He is irrelevant to what is really important in the lives of these people.

2. Jesus sides with government authorities in spite of their oppression of the poor. In which case, God legitimates tyranny.

3. Jesus sides with the poor and the powerless in their struggle against the established order and joins them in their opposition to oppression.

The idea that God might side with the poor and oppressed in their efforts to resist injustice was a whole new way of thinking for my students. The idea that God might side with Marxist revolutionaries against the ruling establishment was hard for them to accept. Going along with Romans 13:13, they had always believed that those who ruled were ordained by God to do so. However, given the options available to these poor people, they changed their minds and most of them agreed that a righteous God would have to stand with the poor in their struggle for justice. "Welcome to Liberation Theology," I said to them.

That, for the sake of justice, God sides with the poor and oppressed against the rich and the powerful is not a perspective owned solely by Liberation Theologians. Indeed, any careful reading of the Bible itself might lead many others to this same conclusion. In the history of Israel, the scriptures tell how, when the Jews found themselves enslaved in Egypt, Yahweh spoke to them and told them that He had heard their cries. The God of the Jews declared Himself to be a God who would fight for them and deliver them from their oppressors and would lead them into the Promised Land.

Later in Israel's history, when the Jews had become established in a land of their own, their God again revealed Himself to be a God who champions the cause of the poor and the oppressed. In the class struggles that took place within the life of Israel, Yahweh again and again showed that He stands with the downtrodden and the weak. Whenever the rich and the powerful made life hard for the poor and oppressed, Yahweh would send His prophets to rail against the perpetrators of suffering.

Whether it was from Isaiah, Jeremiah, Amos, or Micah, the cry was always the same: God expected justice from His people more than anything else. The prophetic message from God is clear:

> He hath shewed thee, O man, what is good; and what doth the LORD require of thee, but to do justly, and to love mercy, and to walk humbly with thy God? (Mic. 6:8)

The New Testament picks up the same theme. The birth of Jesus was heralded by the Virgin Mary, declaring to the world that her Son would be the deliverer for the socially disinherited and would bring hope for those who had no hope:

> And Mary said, My soul doth magnify the LORD,
> And my spirit hath rejoiced in God my Saviour.
> For he hath regarded the low estate of his handmaiden: for, behold, from henceforth all generations shall call me blessed.
> For he that is mighty hath done to me great things; and holy is his name.
> And his mercy is on them that fear him from generation to generation.
> He hath shewed strength with his arm; he hath scattered the proud in the imagination of their hearts.
> He hath put down the mighty from their seats, and exalted them of low degree.
> He hath filled the hungry with good things; and the rich he hath sent empty away.

THE "BOTTOMS UP" REVOLUTION   61

He hath helped his servant Israel, in remem-
brance of his mercy;
As he spake to our fathers, to Abraham, and
to his seed forever. (Luke 1:46–55)

The followers of Jesus preached and wrote the same
message. Certainly the book of James makes it clear that
Yahweh is a God who cannot tolerate the exploitation of
the poor and the oppression of the defenseless by those
who have power and wealth.

Go to now, ye rich men, weep and howl for
your miseries that shall come upon you.
    Your riches are corrupted, and your garments
are motheaten.
    Your gold and silver is cankered; and the rust
of them shall be a witness against you, and
shall eat your flesh as it were fire. Ye have
heaped treasure together for the last days.
    Behold, the hire of the laborers who have
reaped down your fields, which is of you kept
back by fraud, crieth: and the cries of them
which have reaped are entered into the ears of
the LORD of sabaoth. (James 5:1–4)

There are as many as six hundred passages of scripture
that make us aware that God has a special commitment
to the poor. This is because He is a God who loves justice, and it is the poor who are usually the victims of
injustice.

We middle-range Christians buy into this view of
God. And while we are not about to take up arms

against the ruling establishment, we nevertheless work for justice for the oppressed and help the poor. We are part of what futurologist Tom Sine calls "The Mustard Seed Conspiracy." By establishing within our society a variety of programs and projects that express a love and concern for the poor that runs counter to the values of our consumer-oriented society, we believe we can gradually permeate that society with a new ethos. We believe that we can, through our middle-range projects, be what the Bible calls "leaven."

There is a belief among us that the feelings and the thinking of America can be changed this way. We believe ours is also a kind of Liberation Theology, but it is one of positive nonviolent activism that affirms that God is at work in America, transforming it from the bottom up. And we believe that those who participate with God in what He is doing through our middle-range "Mustard Seed" projects will themselves be transformed in the process.

Christians in the nineties want to become personally involved in meeting the needs of suffering people. Their opting for middle-range projects stems from a desire to have hands-on experiences and a longing to see direct results from their efforts. They have begun to discover what happens to them emotionally when they are doing things that make a difference in the lives of people whom they personally know.

Youth leaders are finding that the teenagers in their youth groups experience great spiritual renewal and significant consciousness raising by doing such things as building a small school in a Third World country or running a daily vacation Bible school program on a Native American reservation.

Pastors are discovering that the laity comes alive to the relevance of the gospel when they are personally involved in ministries to the poor and oppressed. Those who are directly involved in tutoring the educationally disadvantaged, working with ghetto delinquents, creating jobs for the unemployed, and caring for the homeless turn out to be the most spiritually zealous of all church members. Praxis, the transformation of personality through involvement in direct social action, is becoming a primary means of converting people into a deeper understanding of the Christian faith.

Carter and Habitat for Humanity

A brilliant example of the shift to middle-range programs for social change can be found in the most recent work of former president Jimmy Carter. Since leaving office, Carter has continued to be active in working for social change on the macro level. He has been negotiating with some of the key leaders of Africa to end wars and to facilitate nation building. He is still a major player in the affairs of the Middle East. His continuous influence in world affairs is such that *Time* magazine now considers him one of the best ex-Presidents we have ever had. Yet, for all of his accomplishments in negotiating social justice and peace in recent years, he has gained his greatest recognition for his work with a Christian missionary organization known as Habitat for Humanity.

Habitat for Humanity is a movement started by a Georgian neighbor to Carter named Millard Fuller. Committed to building houses for poor people who could otherwise never hope to own homes of their own, Fuller organized this movement that now is doing work in over 450 communities across the United States and around the world.

Each day as many as six houses are completed and offered to poor families at only the cost of construction. No down payment is required, and the long-term mortgages provided involve no interest payments. Fuller established this no-interest principle after reading scriptures. He applied the Mosaic doctrine that when money is lent to the poor, it should be done without interest.

> If thou lend money to any of my people that is poor by thee, thou shalt not be to him as an usurer, neither shalt thou lay upon him usury. (Exod. 22:25)

It was permissible, according to his reading of the Bible, to charge the rich interest, because when the rich borrow money it is usually to invest and to make more money. Therefore, it seems only fair to charge interest to the rich so that the lenders can share in the profit. But when the poor borrow money it is usually because they are desperate, and the Bible requires that they not be exploited by those who have the means to help them. This principle became basic to the Habitat for Humanity philosophy.

The price of these housing units is incredibly low. This is primarily because the poor families that buy them are charged only what it costs to build them. Building materials are often donated and volunteers do the construction work. Consequently, poor families can buy homes for themselves with monthly payments that are dramatically less than what they would have to pay if they were renting.

Among those volunteers who drive nails, saw wood, and hang shingles is the former president of the United States. In Philadelphia, New York, Charlotte, Atlanta, and a number of other cities across America, Jimmy Carter's involvement with the work of Habitat for Humanity has brought this organization extensive press coverage and high visibility. It has also enabled Carter to do on the grassroots level what he tried to do as President on the macro level.

In 1975, when Carter initiated his drive for the White House, he chose to do so with a speech he delivered in a burned-out section of the Bronx. Standing on a pile of rubble located on Charlotte Street, he declared that he would make the rebuilding of America's cities a primary goal of his administration.

It did not happen as Carter had hoped. When he left the presidency in 1980, the cities of America were more deteriorated than ever. His macro plan for urban renewal had failed. The attempt to provide decent housing through a government agency did not work as it should have.

Today, Carter is still addressing the same problem— the elimination of substandard housing among the poor. But now he is doing it on the local level. Working through Habitat for Humanity chapters in cities and towns all across America, he is seeing thousands of new homes being built. Working alongside small groups of Christian people, he is bringing about change. He is part of a grassroots reformist movement that is full of hope.

Carter would be the last to say that this effort on the micro level is all that is needed. He is well aware that a comprehensive plan for low-cost housing must be devised by the federal government if American cities are to be rebuilt and slums are to be eliminated. But until such plans are realized, he, like so many other activist Christians, is doing what can be done through direct efforts for people in need.

Fallout from Watergate

Another remarkable example of a person who was involved in ordering society on the macro level and is now focused on grassroots programs is found in Charles Colson. The name is familiar to any who followed the unfolding of the Watergate scandals during the presidency of Richard M. Nixon. Colson was chief counsel for the White House during the Nixon years and, in that position, played a key role in the Watergate cover-up. He was tried, found guilty, and sent to prison.

Something happened to Colson on his way to jail. He became a Christian. Concerned men who live in the Washington area and who call themselves The Fellowship reached out to him during this time of adversity and shared with him their understanding of the gospel. Having nowhere else to turn for help, Colson turned to Christ and found in Him hope and salvation. Colson had what is commonly referred to as a "born-again" experience. His life was radically changed, and he committed himself to Christian service.

It did not take Colson long to discover a mission that would occupy him for years to come. While in prison, he discovered an unmet need. He encountered men and women who had been ignored by the church, pushed around by society, and often forsaken by family and friends. He met fellow prisoners who had failed to get due process from the law. He even found men who did not know why they were in jail. Prison became a place of revelation and calling. He made a decision to do something about all of this, and upon release he founded Prison Fellowship.

The program of Prison Fellowship is relatively simple. It involves getting ordinary Christians to do what they can to express loving concern for those behind bars in their local communities. Within a few years of its inception, laypersons across America were organizing into local chapters of Prison Fellowship. The ministries of these chapters consist of evangelism, personal counseling, and providing whatever help is possible to those in jail. Through evangelistic programs and personal discussions with prisoners, thousands have been led to make commitments to Christ. In cooperation with local churches, arrangements have been worked out to provide the kind of supervised personal care necessary for those released from prison. Church people find them jobs and places to live. Support groups are made available to love and encourage these ex-convicts. Working through local churches, Prison Fellowship has been able to set up a system that minimizes the recidivism among former convicts and helps them to reenter society successfully. All of this is done on the grassroots level.

Prison Fellowship also works for prison reforms. But its efforts to make prison treatment more humane are carried out primarily by Christians working in their own communities. Usually it is through direct discussion with the wardens that those in Prison Fellowship work to bring about changes. While those in Colson's organizations are also diligent in trying to implement progressive reforms in penal policy on both the state and the national levels, they seek change primarily through their local chapters.

A few years ago, I attended a national conference for those doing prison work. I listened attentively and sadly as psychologists, criminologists, law enforcement officers, and members of the judicial system gave reports and expressed opinions. The conference was depressing, to say the least. Speaker after speaker spoke of the hopelessness of their efforts. They told of the near inevitability that those released from prison would repeat their crimes. They explained how prisons, rather than being correctional institutions, were, in reality, schools for crime. I heard how those who go to jail get labeled and molded into criminals and, upon ending their incarceration, live out what they have learned. The reports were defeatist, and those at the conference seemed to exhibit resignation to what the penal system and those who were in it had become.

The one bright spot on the program was the presentation made by those involved with Prison Fellowship. Their spokespersons gave reports of people whose lives had been turned around because of their encounters with Christ. There were even a couple of ex-cons on hand to give testimonies of how Prison Fellowship had led them to salvation. The only thing that surprised me was that all of those present did not immediately sign up with Prison Fellowship. It seemed to me to have the only program that was working.

The Value of the Person in the Workplace

Locally based social change is also evident in the work of Wayne Alderson and his "Value of the Person" movement. In what may be one of the best-kept secrets in contemporary Christendom, Alderson has come up with a way to bring the gospel to bear in labor-management relations. Through his efforts, a significant change has taken place in what goes on between union leaders and corporate CEOs in companies as large as the 3M Corporation, with its thousands of employees, and others such as Shaped Wire, with its fifty employees.

The way Value of the Person started explains a great deal about why it exists. For three years, from 1972 to 1974, Alderson was the vice-president of operations at Pittron Steel in Pittsburgh. When he took over that position, the company was on the verge of bankruptcy with a future that offered little hope for a turnaround. A primary reason for the sad condition of the company was the strained relationships between labor and management. The hostilities generated by strikes and the threat of strikes had taken their toll on the company. Low morale was reflected in poor-quality work. Mutual distrust had crippled Pittron's capacity for production.

The biggest problem, in Alderson's eyes, was the humiliation that the workers of the company had been forced to endure at the hands of the former management team. As far as Alderson was concerned, the employees of Pittron simply were not valued as human beings. He decided that something had to be done to change the human dynamics of the situation. To Alderson, this was not simply a matter of good industrial management but a calling to apply his Christian faith to the affairs of the marketplace.

His first efforts were directed at Sam Piccolo, the president of Local 1306 of the United Steel Workers. Although Alderson was a Presbyterian and Piccolo was a

Roman Catholic, they soon discovered that they had a common spiritual bond. It was in the context of their shared love for Christ that Alderson made what must have seemed to be an outlandish proposal to Piccolo. He suggested that labor and management get together on a daily basis for prayer and Bible study.

It was a risk for Piccolo to accept Alderson's proposal. Union members expect their leaders to be at war with management and to treat them as the enemy. Fraternizing with management creates suspicions among the rank-and-file members and fosters the fear that the leadership has sold them out. Union leaders who are friends with those in management are usually accused of making what are referred to as "sweetheart deals" that result in settling for less than the workers feel they deserve. Nevertheless, the risk was taken and the two men invited anybody who wanted to come to attend a lunch-break chapel program.

From the beginning, these overtly Christian gatherings drew a significant proportion of the work force. Some came out of curiosity. Others came out of suspicion. But a good number came out of deep spiritual need.

Many were tired of the animosities that had haunted their plant. Some had deep personal problems that warranted prayer. Still others came because they longed for the dignity that the sons and daughters of God gain in the context of worship. Most of them were not churchgoers. Few of them considered themselves religious. All of them felt awkward. But they came.

Over the weeks and months that followed, a remarkable change occurred at Pittron. Labor and management still had their differences. Problems still needed to be solved. Anger was still something the Pittron family had to deal with. But trust had begun to grow between these hitherto combatants. An appreciation was developing between those on each side. And, most surprising, the company had begun to turn around. Production was up. Quality control was showing remarkable improvement. Surprisingly, this almost defunct company was beginning to turn a profit.

Unfortunately, this is not one of those "and they lived happily ever after" stories. The profitability of the company made it the target of a takeover, and when Pittron fell into new hands, the new owners brought with them their own management team. Alderson found himself out of a job.

Calvinists who look for the sovereign hand of God in all that happens would have no difficulty explaining this turn of events. Alderson's departure from Pittron freed him to travel around the country telling the story of "The Miracle of Pittron."

It was not long before Alderson got together with another union leader, Lefty Scumaci, and initiated the Value of the Person seminars. Packaging what they had learned from their Pittron experiences, these two men began running seminars for companies across America. Boldly Christian, these seminars bring hitherto warring parties together, help them to confront each other honestly and in love, and encourage the correction of bad situations.

Based on these seminars, remarkable changes have been introduced into the workplace. In the words of one enthusiastic union man, "They are treating me like a person now. They used to treat me like a machine."

Management leaders and union workers are learning to implement biblical principles in their relationships with one another. "Love, Dignity, and Respect" is the motto of the Alderson/Scumaci team, and in the more than one thousand companies to which this team has carried the Value of the Person message, testimonies abound as to how these values have influenced the workplace.

I can personally attest to the validity of the effectiveness of these Value of the Person seminars. I have been a part of them and have witnessed the group dynamics that occur. I have seen tough-looking union leaders break down and cry as they relate the feelings of alienation and humiliation they have experienced at the hands of management. I have witnessed managers asking union members for forgiveness and offering hope for reconciliation. I have listened as managers have talked about the betrayal and cheating they have had to endure at the hands of union workers, and I have watched union leaders repent and ask for forgiveness.

The Value of the Person seminars have a low profile. There is no fanfare in the national press to herald what is being accomplished through them. No television specials describe what Alderson and Scumaci are doing. Nevertheless, working on the local level, they may have done more to facilitate reconciliation between labor and management then all the arbitration boards and programs sponsored by the federal government put together. Undoubtedly, scores of strikes by labor have been prevented and a whole new style of management has been introduced because of the quiet "leavening" influence being exercised by these seminars.

A Summary of Middle-Range Programs

The middle-range approach disregards the grand schemes for social change promoted by the prophetic reformist movements discussed earlier. Instead, it is built on the conviction that small, manageable projects in which Christians can be personally and directly involved are the most promising means for making a difference in the world.

This new style of social action emphasizes changing the world through small groups. It is a style in which Christian people in face-to-face relationships devise plans to implement God's justice in the places where they normally live and work. It is built on the premise that when enough small victories for justice are won in the primary associations in which Christians work, play, and hold membership, these victories will have a cumulative outcome that will affect the macro structures of society. It is a theory of social change that presupposes that the kinds of things that small independent groups can carry out will create ripple effects that gradually will flow through the entire social system.

CHAPTER 5

RUMBLINGS FROM THE UNDER GROUND

F THE MESSAGE OF THE PRO-
phet is needed anywhere, it is needed on the campuses
of this nation. There are students at just about every college and university who concur with the diagnosis that
apathy rules as the predominant psychic condition of
the academic community. The kind of rallies and riots
that marked the sixties are gone and forgotten. What
was once an emotionally upset and angry student population has settled down. And while there have been a
few petitions against apartheid in South Africa and some
isolated forums on environmental issues, there have
been few signs of the revolutionary fervor that was so
evident among students during the Johnson and Nixon
years.

Young men and women are not "dropping out" in
accord with the pleas of the old counterculture gurus.

There is no more talk of "The Greening of America." The likes of radical organizations such as Students for a Democratic Society are no longer visible. For the most part, campus talk has been reduced to what money-making opportunities exist during the summer months and what job placement options there are after graduation.

The antiestablishment anger of the sixties seems to have been replaced by an apathetic careerism. What few protest rallies still occur seem only to mimic those of the turbulent years of the past. As far as the press and the ruling establishment are concerned, these minor upsets are to be largely ignored. If the deadness that marks our consumer-oriented society has manifested itself anywhere over the last decade or so, it has done so in the halls of academia. If indeed the prophet is a messenger from God who weeps over what has happened to God's people, then the prophet would have had much to lament upon visiting the campuses of America during these last few years.

But there are rumblings. In the midst of this pervading collegiate apathy, something new seems to be struggling to live. In the emotional graveyards that are all too common in the world of higher education, there appears to be something vital stirring to be born. It is not easy to discern its form or to understand its nature, but there are inklings. And those inklings are a source of hope. As the homespun American philosopher Yogi Berra once said, "It ain't over 'til it's over!" Before writing off American collegiate youth, we should pay attention to these rumblings and ask if something new and dynamic is about to come out of them. Or, as the biblical prophet asked, "Will these dry bones rise again?"

These rumblings are not couched in the revolutionary rhetoric of the angry sixties. They do not manifest themselves in the kind of "media events" made so popular by the Chicago Eight. They have no shrill-pitched spokespersons or any clear political agenda. But they are there. Those who stop to feel their presence will find them. The rumblings are "not yet," but they are about things that are coming. The prophet of God would rejoice in them and cite them as signs of a coming kingdom. The prophet would say they are signs of the times. The prophet would find them grounds for hope.

Signs of the Times

In San Diego, some students from a Nazarene liberal arts college organize to help people with AIDS. They refurbish a dilapidated house and get furnishings and beds. They join with a local committee composed of Christian business and professional people in opening up a hospice for the victims of this dreaded disease. The gay newspaper in the city writes them up, giving them front-page coverage. The AIDS hospice is referred to by this paper as "The House That Love Built."

In Seattle, Washington, another group of Christian students prevails over objections from some of those in their college's administration and gets part of their dormitory set aside to be a shelter for the homeless. Each evening, they get people off the streets who have no place to sleep to come and be with them in their dormitory. They feed these disinherited strangers and treat them as friends. They do not solve the problems of the homeless, but they do make a difference.

In Chicago, some students from still another Christian liberal arts college spend their weekends rehabilitating houses in the slums to provide low-cost dwellings for the poor. In the middle of an urban ghetto, they create houses of beauty that stand in stark contrast to everything around them. There, in that run-down neighborhood, they establish signs of a coming Kingdom.

A national news network does a special on the changing behavior of college students during spring break. Whereas in former years they all seemed to flock to such resort areas as Palm Springs, California, or Ft. Lauderdale, Florida, there is a rising tendency for some of them to spend this time in community service. Working among the poor in Appalachia or on Native American reservations in Arizona, a new breed of students is demonstrating that it gets its gratification out of helping and giving.

The People of EAPE

The Christian altruistic spirit that is rumbling beneath the surface of our consumeristic society has an almost "ideal type" expression in the program of the Evangelical Association for the Promotion of Education (EAPE), which I head. Serving people who live in the subsidized housing communities of Philadelphia and Camden, New Jersey, EAPE carries out its mission almost completely through the efforts of college-age volunteers. These young people serve full-time without pay. They come from all over the country at their own expense, live together in a large old house that once was an orphanage, and come up with their own money to pay for the food they eat. Nevertheless, they come by the hundreds.

During peak times, there are as many as two hundred of them working with as many as fifteen hundred inner-city poor people on any given day. These EAPE workers run tutorial programs for educationally disadvantaged teenagers and day camps for children who otherwise would have little to keep them occupied. Working along with the adult members of government housing communities, they foster a variety of community organizations. In conjunction with the tenants, they are initiating some small businesses in order to provide much-needed income for welfare families. A thrift shop has been established that not only creates some jobs but also makes available to the community inexpensive clothing and house furnishings. Both a lawn-care business and a pizza business have been established to create employment for teenagers. One of EAPE's most successful ventures is a greeting card business. A half dozen former gang members have been trained by EAPE workers to print and market greeting cards and are selling enough of them to make a decent living.

Businesses like these prove to be difficult enterprises, to say the least. Teenagers who have not been raised on a work ethic and who often are school dropouts have difficulty adapting to the requisites of business. The EAPE volunteers often fail and get discouraged. Yet the efforts go on relentlessly. There is little in the way of giving up among these Christian idealists.

A number of other EAPE services are provided by these collegiate volunteers, ranging from latchkey programs to care for children during after-school hours to job training programs for adults. There is an endless array of clubs, Bible study groups, sports programs, and music groups in the EAPE ministries. And all of these programs and activities are carried out by young people who ask for little more than an opportunity to serve others in the name of Christ. These college students volunteer in such numbers that EAPE is helping to place them in similar work settings in other cities.

There has been almost no press coverage of these self-sacrificing college students and what they are accomplishing. That is the way EAPE staff people like it. Through word of mouth, information about the opportunities to work in the EAPE program is passed on through colleges and universities across the country.

The work force of EAPE is composed both of persons who are radically committed and those who are what I have been calling middle-range Christians. Some have given their lives to inner-city ministry among the poor and have set aside all plans for lucrative establishment-type professions. On the other hand, most of these EAPE workers have volunteered for only two years of service and are planning to go back into mainstream employment when their time is up.

EAPE is yet another example of change at the grass-roots level. Its approach to social change has nothing to do with seizing power and imposing "improvements" from the top down. Instead, its collegiate volunteers are attempting to serve on the neighborhood level. They hope that the influences from what is accomplished there will permeate upward through the social system. They believe that macro change can start with micro projects.

Middle-Range Work in the Professions

Professional people also are picking up the prophetic message and opting to break the hold that our consumer-oriented society has had on them. Some do it radically; one example is an accountant I knew who worked in a firm that would have made him rich but gave up his job to work in an orphanage in Cambodia. Like many others, he had grown tired of tiptoeing through life in order to arrive at death safely. He wanted the splendid exhilaration that belongs to those who dare to bet their lives on the cause of the Kingdom.

Most middle-range Christians adopt countercultural values only halfway and would be the first to admit that they have a long way to go to live out fully the call of Christ to forsake all. But they too have their reward.

Once, while preaching in West Virginia, I had a couple of young lawyers in the congregation. My topic that evening was the cost of discipleship. When I gave the invitation for people to commit themselves fully to Christian service, these men did not come forward. Nevertheless, they did accept the challenge to alter their lives and seek ways in which they could more fully serve Christ and the poor.

These two men practiced law together, and they made a decision to offer free legal services to poor people who lived in their county. This was a decision to go way beyond the set amount of *pro bono* work (work without charge) that most law firms do. These men decided to help anyone in the county who needed their help.

Their commitment to the poor changed their lives dramatically. Not only did they become known as friends of the poor, but their good reputation brought in an avalanche of unexpected new paying customers. What was even more encouraging was that scores of people who were delinquent in the payment of fees suddenly paid up. "I suppose they didn't want to cheat lawyers who helped the poor," one of these young men explained.

They still have their BMWs, they still vacation in Bermuda, and they still have a lot of the things that "worldly" people in our consumer-oriented society make the essence of their lives. They haven't given it all up for Jesus. But they are prime examples of middle-range Christians who are doing *something* significant for Christ in their everyday lives. They are not simply slaves to the system.

If you are not going to drop everything and follow Jesus, then you, like these lawyers, ought to be asking yourself what you can be doing right where you are. Some of us, as they say, have to bloom where we are planted. For instance, if you are an accountant, look around for those charitable organizations that need somebody to audit their books. With the new levels of fiscal accountability being demanded of Christian organizations by both the government and the general public, there is probably a missionary program or a youth ministry close to where you live and work that desperately needs your help.

There is a banker I know who was all too aware of the fact that banks are reluctant to lend money to poor people. (Harry S. Truman once said that banks are institutions that lend money to people who can prove they don't need it.) This man responded to the call of Christ by setting up a savings and loan association that specializes in lending money to the poor. He has worked out a system whereby poor people are linked up with economically successful people he has recruited from churches. The latter assume responsibility to serve as consultants to the poor, showing them what goes into being financially responsible. For the poor who need money for things like buying a house or setting up a small business, getting the loan is contingent upon their willingness to enter into such an arrangement. The results have been most encouraging.

Poor people who were bad risks "on paper" have paid back their loans. Many people who did not know how to handle money have learned to do so. It isn't anything that makes the headlines, but what Robert Lavelle is doing is part of that Mustard Seed Conspiracy that can change America and bring it back to life.

In rural Pennsylvania, there are a couple of auto mechanics who decided to use their skills for the Kingdom of God. They have set up a small, nonprofit organization that fixes up cars for Christian organizations. I do not know what we at EAPE would do without their help. They have made several cars and station wagons available for our use. These vehicles are absolutely essential for our work with inner-city children. And we are only one of scores of organizations that have expanded their ministries to needy people because of the commitment of these auto mechanics.

My friend Ron Barbaro, a top executive with The Prudential Insurance Company, had heard me speak on several occasions and knew of my concern that Christians respond with help for people who are dying of AIDS.

Time and time again I had painted verbal pictures in public addresses of the failure of the church and our society to provide the compassionate care that people with AIDS need.

Ron pulled me aside one day after I had spoken and told me of a new policy that he had instituted with Prudential. He had made it possible for people who have AIDS to collect on their life insurance policies *before* they were dead. To Prudential it was no gigantic giveaway. The company would have had to pay the money sooner or later. But because of this new policy, those suffering with AIDS would be able to pay for their medical care and for other services to make their lives a little more bearable.

Ron explained to me, "I saw too many cases in which a family would abandon a guy with AIDS only to pick up his insurance check when he died. I thought to myself that the dying guy should have had that money. So I decided to make that kind of thing happen." This is one more example of somebody making things different by putting life and feeling into a business.

Pete and Sue Carter were my students at Eastern College. During their college years, they got involved in ministry with street kids in the Kensington section of Philadelphia. They got "hooked" on what they were doing, and when they graduated from college, they went to live in the neighborhood where they had been working. They bought a house in a run-down community, took available jobs close by, and made being a presence for Christ in what could be called a very bad neighborhood their primary mission in life.

It was not long before the teenagers who had come to know them began hanging out at their house. A few of the street kids who had no homes of their own came to live with Pete and Sue.

The effect that these two young people are having on the youth of Kensington is hard to measure. But I am convinced that they are more of the "Salt of the Earth" that Jesus has called us to be. I know that they are part of what God is doing to give new life to a dying America.

On the Individual Level

Perhaps one of the best examples I know of extraordinary service for the Kingdom of God being done on the micro level is the story of a young woman named Nancy. I met Nancy because she was a guest on a radio show that I host on WZZD in Philadelphia. Nancy is crippled and confined to a wheelchair, yet she has developed a unique ministry to hurting and lonely people of the city. It is beautiful in its simplicity. She runs ads in the personals section of the newspaper that read:

> If you are lonely or have a problem call me. I am in a wheelchair and seldom get out. We can share our problems with each other. Just call. I'd love to talk.

The results are astounding. Each week at least thirty calls come in. She spends her days comforting and counseling people. She has become someone to lean on for hundreds of people with problems.

When I asked Nancy how she became crippled, she answered, "By trying to commit suicide."

I was stunned. She went on to explain, "I was living alone. I had no friends. I hated my job, and I was constantly depressed. I decided to jump from the window of my apartment, but instead of being killed, I ended up in the hospital paralyzed from my waist down. The second night I was in the hospital, Jesus appeared to me and told me that I'd had a healthy body and a crippled soul but from then on I would have a crippled body and a healthy soul. I gave my life to Christ right there and then.

"When I got out of the hospital, I tried to think of how a woman like me in a wheelchair could do some good, and I came up with the idea of putting the ad in the newspaper. And the rest, as they say, is all history."

Following Father Abraham

In all of this talk about revolutionizing America by infusing it with new spiritual vitality and challenging our consumer-oriented life-style, we have not paid much attention to our so-called senior citizens. There is a tendency to assume that, after age fifty, people are not likely to make the bold moves or engage in the daring things that can shake the foundations of society and prepare the way for a new day and a new kind of world. But that notion is now being challenged.

What I like about the biblical story of Abraham and Sarah is that God called them to the mission of changing the world when they were old people (Hebrews 11). Abraham responded to the call when "his life was far spent," and Sarah joined in the mission "when she was past age." Imagine Abraham at ninety-four waking up one morning and shaking Sarah, his ninety-two-year-old wife, with the news, "Sarah! Sarah! Get up! We're going to create a new humanity! A new nation! A new epoch in human history!"

The poor woman probably rolled over in her bed as she mumbled, "Go back to bed, Abe. You're confused."

"No, Sarah," he might have answered, "I had this dream. God told me! You and I are going to start a whole new race and give birth to a whole new nation!"

"How does this new race start?" Sarah must have sleepily inquired.

"Glad you asked," said Abraham, with a sly little grin on his lips. And they both fell back in bed laughing.

The next scene is Abraham and Sarah, his ninety-two-year-old wife, leaving Ur of the Chaldeans, Abraham "not knowing whither he went" as "he looked for a city which hath foundations, whose builder and maker is God" (Heb. 11:8, 10).

"Where are you going?" their amused neighbors might have shouted out to them.

"We don't know," would have been the answer.

"Well, what do you intend doing when you get to this place you don't know about?" they might have taunted.

"We're going to build a new nation. We're going to give birth to a new people. We're going to give humanity a new beginning," the old folks would have shouted back.

Oh, that we had a host of people like Abraham and Sarah. Oh, that the millions of so-called retired people of America would wake up to God's calling.

With early retirement becoming more and more the norm, we are confronted with the astounding fact that 32 percent of all men between the ages of fifty-five and sixty-four are already retired and on pensions. With all of these human resources who are financially independent and who have lifetimes of experience, you would think that there would be an endless stream of volunteers for the work of the Kingdom. You would think that the tutoring programs in the ghettos and the ministries to the homeless would not be able to handle all the people lined up to serve. Such is not the case. Once retired, these people simply drop out. A lot of them go to Florida and Arizona to relax. They claim that they have done their part and are now going to take it easy.

I would like to remind retired people that only once is retirement talked about in the Bible.

> And he spake a parable unto them, saying, The ground of a certain rich man brought forth plentifully: And he thought within himself, saying, What shall I do, because I have no room where to bestow my fruits: And he said, This will I do: I will pull down my barns, and build greater; and there will I bestow all my fruits and my goods. And I will say to my soul, Soul, thou hast much goods laid up for many years; take thine ease, eat, drink, and be merry. But God said unto him, Thou fool, this night thy soul shall be required of thee: then whose shall those things be, which thou hast provided? So is he that layeth up treasure for himself, and is not rich toward God. (Luke 12:16–21)

The work of God in America needs these senior citizens if we are to break the demonic hold that consumerism has on us. The last part of life cannot be seen as merely a time to treat ourselves to all of the things that society says we need in order to be happy. Life is meant to be more than traveling around in recreational vehicles towing boats. The seemingly endless days of

retirement were not all meant to be spent on golf courses and in fishing boats.

There is growing evidence that the elderly segment of
the population is quickly becoming the most self-cen-
tered, self-serving group of people in America. Rather
than being a blessing, they are becoming more and more
of a drag on the younger population. And there seem to
be more of them every day.

Fortunately, some are rebelling against the stereotypi-
cal roles for retired people. There are Barb and Phil
Julian, who retired from a career in the U.S. Navy to join
the staff of EAPE. These two "retired" people work day
and night in our programs with youth. Having raised ten
children of their own, they are well equipped to provide
the stability that comes with maturity for our many
young volunteers and staff workers. Recently, the
Julians have been joined by a middle-aged divorced
woman and a widow. These two women come from professional backgrounds and bring expertise in business
and education, as well as willing spirits and loving
hearts, to our ministries.

Trevor's Place, a nationally known program for the
homeless, is getting an increasing number of volunteers
from the retirement community of Philadelphia. As a
matter of fact, two of my own aunts who are in their
seventies work at Trevor's Place almost daily.

President Carter's mother, Lillian, established a solid
example for service by joining the Peace Corps as a
senior citizen. Now thousands of older people are following her example.

These are rumblings of something new. There are
inklings of a new beginning. There is hope that a group
of drowsy people will wake up to their potentialities and

help to awaken a nation. Those who are old must dream dreams, even as the Scripture says. They must realize that life was not made for consumerism or retirement. They must learn that life was made for living, and that living is serving. They must come to see that life was meant to be more than a walk between two hospitals—the one for birth and the one for death. The hour is at hand when people must come into the fullness of their humanity and rebel against the ways that society has prescribed for them to retire. They should follow instead the lead of Abraham and Sarah.

CHAPTER 6

THE CHURCH IS ALIVE AND WELL AND LIVING IN AMERICA

PROPHETS HAVE NEVER GOTTEN on well with organized religion. In ancient Israel, they picked on the priests who pretended to be the official spokesmen for God and accused them of being phonies. Jesus had less-than-harmonious relations with the priests and scribes of His day. And since His time, prophetic voices have kept up their barrage of attacks on the officially ordained servants who dress in clerical garb.

The accusations seem to have a sameness to them. The religious professionals are generally condemned for being more interested in holding on to their jobs than they are in speaking the truth.

Søren Kierkegaard, who was a specialist in picking on the clergy, once said:

> It is one thing to love humanity so much that you are willing to die on a cross to save humanity. It is quite another to expect to earn a big

salary describing a somebody who died to save
humanity.*

Of course there is always much for prophets to find
wrong with the religious establishment. To gain power
and wealth, the clergy have regularly made peace with
kings and presidents, giving their blessings when they
should have been declaring the judgments of God. To fill
their pews, preachers have too often told people what
they wanted to hear instead of exposing their sinful
ways. The religious establishment is commonly accused
of compromising the truth in order to gain favor and
praise. And church leaders, for political and economic
reasons, have given "the right hand of fellowship" to
people who should have gotten a kick in the pants.
Undoubtedly the Old Testament prophets would go hard
on our American churches should they speak to us
today.

A young Jewish student I knew who had been converted to Christianity once expressed his disappointment
with the church by telling me, "If somebody took Jesus's
teachings in the Beatitudes (Matt. 5:3–12) and decided to
create a religion that contradicted those teachings, then
he'd probably come up with the Protestant church."

While that judgment is far too harsh, there is some
truth to it. Whereas Jesus taught that the poor are
blessed, the church often suggests that living like a
Christian is a way to financial success. Whereas Jesus
taught, "Blessed are they that mourn," we seem to

---

*Søren Kierkegaard, *Attack upon "Christendom,"* Princeton, NJ: Princeton Univ.
Press, 1944.

promise happiness and smiles. Church people tend to support capital punishment instead of mercy. And we are more known for supporting a strong military than we are for being peacemakers. Undoubtedly, we church people too often adopt a life-style that is aimed at winning friends and influencing people rather than one that might lead to persecution.

There is little doubt that any real prophet who looked at the contemporary church would get on our case most for our apparent capitulation to the value system of our consumer-oriented society. For the most part, we have remained silent in the face of the seductiveness of American affluence and have had little to say about the sinful things that we as a nation do to make our way of life possible.

Prophets would rail against what we have done to the environment in order to maintain our cars and produce the things we have been conditioned to want. They would hit us hard for our willingness to support oppressive dictators in Third World countries simply because they serve our economic interests. But most of all, they would condemn us for allowing our spiritual hungers to be replaced by the craving for things that has become the hallmark of our consumerism.

The Radical Church of the Prophets

All across America, there are people who share the concerns that the prophets of God would have. These are the radical disciples who lead the way in establishing a countercultural church that dares to declare the judgment of God upon the nation.

Perhaps the best example of this church is found in the Sojourners Community in Washington, DC. Led by Jim Wallis, one of the most articulate preachers in America, this congregation has taken the lead in exposing hypocrisy in government and superficiality in Christendom. The members of the Sojourners Community have earned a reputation for being radically opposed to U.S. policy on apartheid in South Africa, on nuclear weapons, and on the war in El Salvador. They can be counted on to be supporters of feminist issues as well as justice for gays and lesbians. They don't just talk. They march. They live dangerously.

Against our consumer-oriented society, these people have made an alternative life-style one of the cannons of their faith. The call of Christ, as far as they are concerned, requires that we live simply so that others might simply live. Their message to the rest of us is to cut back on buying things that are not needed and to adopt measures that are ecologically responsible. Such stances, they claim, are some of the things that go with being a Christian. They are not options.

The Sojourners Community, in many ways, serves as a conscience for the rest of the churches of America. The people of this group will not let us forget that justice issues are at the core of the gospel. Through the publication of their magazine, they keep us aware of what the government is doing that we, as Christians, should be questioning. They represent a form of Christianity that will not be at home with the ruling political establishment but, instead, constantly judges the government on the basis of the teachings of the Bible. What is more important, they make it clear that we Christians too easi-

ly support the injustices of the political-economic system, precisely because that system guarantees that we
can have the consumeristic life-style that has seduced us
all.

The Sojourners Community does not stand alone. It is
only a prototype. I know of churches very much like it
in cities as large as Chicago and Philadelphia and in
towns as small as Americus, Georgia. There are some
who estimate that there are hundreds of these groups
throughout America, who regularly come together to
worship and to strengthen one another to stand against
the culture.

American Christianity very much needs the creative
tension created by prophetic countercultural churches
such as the Sojourners community. The nation needs to
be challenged by such radical followers of Christ to
wake up to what is happening to its people. The prophet
of God would probably be happiest in fellowship with
them and would resonate most to their message.

The Church of the Oppressed

There is another church in America that also would
attract the prophet. It too stands apart from the social
system and challenges its sins. It stands apart from society not by choice but because it has been pushed there
by the people of the ruling establishment. This, of
course, is the church of the oppressed. It is the church
that gathers together the socially disinherited and gives
them a voice.

As a teenager, some of my African-American school-
mates took me to the Mt. Olivet Baptist Church in

Philadelphia to hear their preacher, Marshall Shepard, Sr.
I had not experienced his kind of preaching before. What
he had to say that morning seemed more related to the
existential situation of blacks in America than any other
sermon I had heard before. He talked of Shadrach,
Meshach, and Abednego, those ancient Jewish youths
who, while in slavery, refused to bend to the pressures
and demands of their masters. Even now I can hear him
explaining how these Old Testament heroes, when told
to give up the names given to them by their ancestors,
refused to do so. They refused, said Shepard, even though
it meant being thrown into "the fiery furnace." He
rhetorically asked from his pulpit:

> Can you imagine those young men being will-
> ing to die rather than give up the names of their
> fathers? Can you understand these young men
> who would sooner die than to give up who they
> really were and to forget where they had origi-
> nally come from? Can you identify with these
> slaves who would not surrender their identities
> nor adopt for themselves the last names of their
> masters?

There were shouts of "Yes!" and "All right now!" All
over the congregation there were people becoming aware
that God's people must not deny who they are or ever
capitulate to a culture that really is not their own. The
people in that Sunday morning congregation were finding in Shepard's message the Biblical support for their
efforts to reaffirm their African heritage and to stand fast
against those who would make them into something
other than they really were. This was anything but good

hermeneutics, and it was not even a fair interpretation
of what really happened in the Bible story, but it certainly was good preaching!

The climax of Shepard's sermon focused on Moses,
and it did so in such a way that it made that Old Testament patriarch a prototype for every African-American
man and woman caught up in the identity struggles that
go with living in a predominantly white society. He told
how Moses, the son of a slave, ended up living in the
"big mansion house" of the Pharaoh. He explained how
Moses came to be taught the ways of the Egyptians so
that he ended up "dressing and talking just like one of
them."

But then Shepard went on to relate how, as a young
man, Moses came upon an Egyptian soldier beating and
kicking a poor, demoralized Jewish slave. Using the
vocabulary and idioms of Philadelphia street language,
Shepard half shouted and half screamed at the congregation:

> But when Moses saw what was happenin' he
> knew. Somethin' down deep inside told him
> who he was and where he came from. Somethin'
> down deep inside made him know that he was
> one with that Jew and "The Man"—you know
> what I mean—I mean "The Man"—you know—
> the man with the whip—that Egyptian man
> who always is out there making life hard for
> you—that man—is the enemy, and has to die.

The congregation was alive with shouts of agreement.
Some were clapping. Others were shouting. There were
cries for the preacher to "Go on now!"

Everyone there knew that he was talking not just about a Hebrew man who had lived thousands of years ago. They knew he was talking about each of them and what was going on in their own lives. There, in that church, there was little doubt about what the preacher was telling his people to do and be. And being the only white person in that two-thousand-plus gathering, I was more than a bit uncomfortable.

Jesus As a "Nigger"

While Black Liberation Theology can be heard in some form or another from most African-American pulpits, it has gained its best-known expression in the preaching and writing of James Cone. I got a firsthand taste of Cone's message and what he could do to an audience when I once heard him speak at a chapel service at a small Christian college. The predominantly white audience had come with wary anticipation, having heard of Cone's reputation. They sat in dead silence as this teacher in the field of black theology took the rostrum. With his eyes flashing and his voice raised, Cone started his sermon with a line designed to shock them:

"Jesus is a nigger!" he shouted. "And all who would be His followers must be ready to become niggers, too."

The impact was electric. The mostly white audience sat stunned at what had sounded like blasphemy and was, in the minds of most, certainly obscenity. But Cone went on to clarify his statement and to leave most of us convinced that he was right. He explained that, if what we mean by "nigger" is not just a black person, but rather one who is despised, rejected, spat upon, and treated like trash...then Jesus was a nigger. The fifty-third chapter of Isaiah, he claimed, said as much.

There was little room for argument when he finished his explanation. Few rebuttals could be offered. There was an obvious biblical basis for his claims. There was only a stunned acceptance of what he had dared to say.

It is not just black theologians who declare that to be a Christian is to identify with the Christ, who Himself identified with the wretched and oppressed of the world. It is not just Cone who would argue that to follow Jesus is to join in the struggle to throw off the chains of inferiority and humiliation and to become part of a movement that brings dignity to all peoples. To be a Christian, many would say, is to join in a revolution. And if that revolution turns violent, it will be the violence of the oppressors who want to "keep black people in their place" that sets off the spark. To the likes of Cone, the time of quiet endurance is over. The time of silent suffering is over. The day of the Lord is at hand!

Women As Oppressed Christians

We need not go to minority groups like the African-American community to find a people with whom a prophet can identify. There is a group of oppressed people *within* the mainstream of American Christianity that is beginning to rise up in righteous indignation against the church and against society. I am referring to women.

Until the last decade, women in the church did not see themselves as a persecuted group. But all of that has changed. Today there is a growing consciousness among women that they have been denied fair treatment and equality by the male-dominated hierarchies of Christendom. They are rejecting inferior status and the traditional roles that have been assigned to them and are challenging the system with angry demands that things be changed.

In our consumer-oriented, male-chauvinistic society, women have generally been defined as shoppers. Men have been the ones who make the money and their wives, the ones who spend it. Thorsten Veblen, one of the dominant thinkers in sociology and economics in the early part of this century, pointed out that, in America, men were so busy making money that they had no time to spend it. Consequently, men could not buy those things that would signal to others their successful status. That is one reason, said Veblen, that men needed wives. Wives could be "the conspicuous consumers," as Veblen called them, and could buy and parade the clothes, cars, and decorated homes that would show off how successful their husbands had become.

I do not dismiss the Veblen thesis lightly. There is no doubt in my mind that America has tended to force a definition upon women that has them thinking of themselves primarily as consumers. If the consumer-oriented society is one in which people think that what is really important in life comes with buying things, then women were the first to be duped into this mentality.

Millard Fuller, the founder of Habitat for Humanity, tells of having become a millionaire by the age of twenty-nine. He had, he says, bought his wife "everything" she possibly could want. But one day he came home to a note that announced that she had left him.

Millard went after her and caught up with her on a Saturday night in a hotel in New York City. They talked into the wee hours of the next morning as she poured out her heart and made him see that the "things" that our consumer-oriented society says are supposed to be so satisfying had left her cold. Her heart was empty and her spirit was burned out, she explained. She was dead inside and she wanted to live again. Kneeling at their bedside in that hotel room, Millard and Linda decided to sell everything they had and dedicate themselves to serving poor people and to working for justice for the oppressed.

The next day being Sunday, they found the nearest Baptist church and went there to worship and thank God for their new beginning. They got to church early, hunted up the minister, and told him about what had happened to them and the decision they had made.

To their surprise, the minister told them that such a radical decision was not really necessary. "He told us that it was not necessary for us to give up everything," Millard said. "He just didn't understand that we weren't giving up money and the things that money could buy. We were giving up a whole way of life that was killing us."

Today the Fullers are two of the most alive people I know. As they work toward making affordable housing available for the poor, they do so with boundless energy. They have broken the psychic spell that American consumerism puts on people. They have "mounted up like eagles." In a hotel room in New York, they were "born again."

I tell this story because I believe it is symptomatic of what is happening more and more across America, and especially within our churches. Women are rising up and letting it be known that having a checking account and a credit card is not enough for them. They are crying out for a chance to invest their lives in ways that have spiritual significance. They are demanding the opportunity to do those things that take away the deadness of their souls. They will no longer tolerate the numbness of the spirit that comes from being without heroic options to live out.

The women's movement in the church is much more than a crusade to gain the right of ordination for women (although this is symbolic of what it is all about). It is more than an attempt to get inclusive language into hymn books. And it transcends the demand of women to control their biological destinies. It is a call for liberation from what the church and society have done to them. It is an attack on all those cultural barriers to the full realization of their humanity. Women will not be satisfied with equal pay for equal work (although they will settle for nothing less). Their aspirations for life cannot be bought off with mink coats and a Mercedes.

In reality the women's movement in the church is a rebellion against what our consumer-oriented society is all about. That, of course, is why the women's movement is so important to the church. As women explode the myths of our culture and show us what is of ultimate significance, they stand a chance of dragging the rest of us along with them. We may go kicking and screaming, but we will go, nevertheless.

What women will gain in their struggle for cultural liberation will not only bless them—it will bless all of us male chauvinists who have given them such a hard time and called them degrading names. It just may be that the revival that the church needs if it is to challenge the psychic slavery and deadness of America will come from women. The prophet who delivers us from our consumer-oriented mind-set could well be a prophetess.

CHAPTER 7

SOME OLD WINE IN SOME NEW WINE SKINS

MANY, IF NOT MOST, OF those who go to church are on a personal survival course. The spiritual death of the nation may be a serious problem, and the need for a prophetic call to repentance may be a crucial necessity, but so many in the Sunday morning congregation have other concerns. They are trying to hold themselves and their families together. Some are struggling to keep empty-shell marriages from falling apart. Others are worried about their alienated kids who are dressing punk and probably doing drugs. There are divorced mothers whose angry children seem out of control. And then there is the man whose alcoholic wife is drinking herself to death. Such people are ready to leave to others the job of assisting at the rebirth of a nation. The wretched poor of the world may desperately need their help, but their own spiritual poverty and the emotional needs of those who are closest to them are what overwhelms most churchgoers. They do not want a church that challenges them to change the world. Instead, they are looking for a church that will comfort them and bind up their wounds. They come to church weary and ready to cry, and they want help. Enter the superchurch!

Unlike the typical mainline churches, which are considered more than healthy if they have three to four hundred in attendance at every Sunday morning worship service, superchurches have congregations that can number in the thousands. I have preached in one superchurch that registers more than fifteen thousand at their weekly worship service (they have three services to accommodate the crowds). Already in America, according to John Vaughan of the International Megachurch Research Center at Southwest Baptist University, there are 270 churches with average weekly congregations of more than two thousand. And a new church joins this group every two to three weeks. These churches are the wave of the future, because they are equipped to meet the variety of needs that are everywhere evident in our stressed-out society.

The prophets and those churches that they inspire may be endeavoring to call the society to repentance and to convert people from the consumer-oriented life-styles that have made us such a messed-up generation. But, in the meantime, the victims of our consumeristic way of life need help, and it is the superchurches that seem best able to provide it.

Because superchurches are so large, they have the resources to provide the host of special services and programs that people believe they must have in order to "make it" in their everyday lives. In one superchurch I visited in Southern California, there are courses in parenting, a special ministry to divorced persons, a support group for parents of homosexuals, programs on how to handle codependence, and other specialized study groups too numerous to list. The place is a religious supermarket. All of these programs are of high quality. Each has a specially trained professional leader. These programs are in addition to what this church considers its "regular" program, which offers the following:

1. *A Singles Program.* This includes a weekly meeting that brings together between three hundred and five hundred business and professional singles to hear an outstanding speaker and to socialize. There are special Sunday school classes geared to the needs of single persons, and a variety of social outings. There are weekend "spiritual renewal" retreats and ski retreats. There are outreach programs that offer singles the opportunities to visit shut-ins, build low-cost housing for the poor, go on short-term mission trips to Third World countries, and engage in a host of other challenging ways to serve the less fortunate. Two full-time ministers are provided to supervise these activities and to offer special counseling to singles who are having personal problems. This ministry is designed for singles from twenty-five to thirty-five years of age, and participants can meet Christians who are potential marital partners.

2. *A College and Career Program.* In many ways this program is like the one offered to singles, but the emphasis here is on college-age youth. The music and speakers for the weekly meetings are all geared to be rel-

evant to young people in this age bracket. Full-time ministers who have special expertise in working with college-age youth give leadership to this program, and the church provides an operating budget that is well over $100,000 per year.

3. *High School and Jr. High School Programs.* Allowing no cost to stand in its way, this superchurch has hired the experts in ministry to teenagers. They know that parents are desperate to find churches that will do something for these young people. Christian rock musicians are frequently brought in for special concerts. Films, specially produced for teenagers, are regularly shown. The array of rallies, conferences, retreats, and conventions that these young people are taken to regularly would be far too long to list.

4. *Sports Programs.* This church has its own gym and a full-time sports director who makes sure that there are leagues for almost every sport and for just about every age group. There are a variety of sports banquets for handing out trophies for winners and regular "chapels" in which Christian principles are applied to athletics.

5. *Music Programs.* This church has five full-time musicians on its staff. There are youth choirs, children's choirs, bell choirs, an orchestra, and gospel quartets to go along with its regular chancel choir. The music produced is polished with professional skill. The choir is so good that during the Christmas season they put on a special program called "The Singing Christmas Tree." More than a dozen performances of this program play to sold-out crowds that number more than ten thousand at each performance.

6. *Home Bible Studies*. Every member of the church is urged to be part of a home Bible study group that usually meets weekly. Thousands of church members attend these meetings conducted by professional ministers who have made small-group ministry the focus of their energies. Members often find that these small groups become caring communities that love them and look after them in special ways. It is fair to say that the personal attention and pastoral care that is received in these small home Bible studies (usually numbering between fifteen and twenty) rivals what can be found under the auspices of the smaller churches that claim to make such concerns their forte.

7. *Counseling Services*. This particular church has three full-time counselors on its staff. Trained in the skills of psychotherapy, and having integrated their counseling techniques with Biblical principles, these counselors are able to provide expert help to people with marriage problems, troubled teenagers, those who face career crises, and many others.

Ordinary Churches Are Out of the Running

Already, many pastors of ordinary traditional churches feel threatened by these superchurches. One of my former students who interviewed for the pastorate of a Baptist church of 350 members, located in the suburbs of Chicago, told me, "You wouldn't believe what the pulpit committee was expecting of me. They wanted me to guarantee them that I could be a polished preacher, an effective youth leader, an expert family counselor, a good fund-raiser, and a clever business manager, as well as being able to provide leadership in an extensive program of visitation evangelism." This pulpit committee was expecting one man to enable them to compete with all the services and programs being offered by a whole team of ministers and other professionals at the superchurch in the same community.

Superchurches simply outclass ordinary churches. Vaughan suggests that they are a whole new development in Christianity that will change forever what Americans expect that churches will do for them. I am convinced that traditional mainline churches will decline in size and importance in the face of this competition.

Among the various staff members of a superchurch in my Philadelphia suburb there is one full-time minister who does nothing but minister to the children of broken marriages. A divorcee I know who was going to the local Methodist church transferred her membership to this superchurch. She told me, "I had to do it. Raising two boys alone is more than I can handle. Ralph (the special pastor for children of divorced parents) gives me some help, and I need all the help that I can get."

I want to make clear that I believe that this kind of Christianity has provided personal salvation for millions of people who found no solace within ordinary churches. Millions who otherwise would have been lost souls have established a deep relationship with Christ in the context of these superchurches. These churches are havens for yuppies in the midst of a heartless world. They are places where fearful parents find programs that excite their anomic teenagers. These churches express the kind of Christianity that has kept millions from giving up on God.

However, *this kind of religion will not bring about*

social change. Its preachers are not the prophets who will lead the American people to weep over what they have become. As a matter of fact, these preachers will leave the young upwardly mobile professionals in their congregations quite content with their BMWs, Reebok sneaks, and expensive ski weekends. They will not challenge the socioeconomic structures that wreak havoc for so many in the world. And they certainly will not proclaim an alternative vision for the future that might lead Americans to abandon their comfortable life-styles to participate in creating another kind of world.

They preach a kind of religion that will enable people to enjoy a happy state of consciousness in a society that is dying. If America is to change, if Western society is to have a future, and if we as a people are to experience a new birth, something more is needed.

The Prophets and the Superchurches

The prophets would be hard on the superchurches. They would claim that such churches only help people to become better adjusted to our consumer-oriented society instead of calling them to reject it. They would argue that these churches are part of the problem, because they strive to make people comfortable in a society that has gone mad. As far as the prophets are concerned, the affluent middle-class world of America has lost its soul, and churches should be judging it as "wanting," not sanctifying it as a system in which Christians can live.

Undoubtedly, the prophets would seethe over the sermons they would hear in the superchurches. These sermons, they would claim, are misleading because they present an incomplete version of God. The preachers of

the superchurches would be condemned because they
leave out some of the disturbing things that the God of
the biblical prophets have to say to us.

Allow me to generalize by saying that the God of the
superchurches is a God who does not threaten the established order. He is a God who does not cry out against
the injustices of the social system or challenge the
socioeconomic arrangements that sustain those injustices. He is not a God who calls into question the ways
of those who hold wealth and power.

The God that the superchurches describe is a God
who seems almost exclusively interested in the personal
lives of people. He is a God who enables individuals to
escape poor self-images and to achieve the actualization
of their human potentialities. But to the preachers of the
superchurches, he is a God who remains apolitical on
issues such as the war in Central America, the oppression of blacks in South Africa, the absence of adequate
health services for the poor, the destruction of the natural environment, and the injustices of American foreign
policy in the Middle East. Superchurch preachers offer
great sermons about Jesus being a personal Savior, but
they are not about to spell out the socioeconomic impli-
cations of what it means to establish His Kingdom here
on earth. For them, he is a God who stands aloof from
the affairs of governments and multinational corporations and concentrates on helping people to enjoy personal salvation in the here and hereafter.

I do not want in any way to suggest that the biblical
Jesus does not enable us to realize our highest potentialities as persons or that Christianity does not make having
a personal salvation experience with Christ an essential

part of its message. Quite the opposite. I am convinced that a number of mainline denominations have seen the memberships of many of their churches decline in part because they have neglected these crucial dimensions of the gospel.

People need personal salvation. They need a personal mystical oneness with the resurrected Christ. They need the psychological wholeness and the emotional well-being that accompanies becoming new persons in Christ. However, the God of the Bible not only concerns Himself with establishing a personal saving relationship with His Son but also is committed to social justice for all the peoples of the world. The biblical Jesus not only is desperate to help lost sinners "find themselves" but also wills to express the righteousness of Heaven in the context of those social institutions wherein we must live our lives.

It is this social side of the Savior that the prophets probably would argue that the preachers in the super-churches ignore. It is this activist Jesus, who is at work transforming the social order into one that reflects His justice, that they probably would be accused of keeping concealed. The Gospel of Matthew says:

But when Jesus [knew the Pharisees were plotting against him], he withdrew himself from thence: and great multitudes followed him, and he healed them all;

And charged them that they should not make him known:

That it might be fulfilled which was spoken by Isaiah the prophet, saying,

"Behold my servant, whom I have chosen; my
beloved, in whom my soul is well pleased: I
will put my Spirit upon him, and he shall show
judgment to the Gentiles.

He shall not strive, nor cry; neither shall any
man hear his voice in the streets.

A bruised reed shall he not break, and smok-
ing flax shall he not quench, till he send forth
judgment unto victory.

And in his name shall the Gentiles trust"
(Matt. 12:15–21).

But this side of what Jesus is about is purposefully
ignored in the superchurches.

The Sermons of Superchurches

Superchurches are nondenominational and apolitical.
The ministers who have engineered their development
have made sure that they avoid the controversial. They
are theologically evangelical, but they avoid being fundamentalist. The variety of do's and don't's so characteris-
tic of traditional Fundamentalism is arduously avoided.
Sermons against dancing, drinking booze, or other
"evils," so much a part of the topical repertoire of old-
time Fundamentalist pulpit thumpers, are just not
preached. It is not that the pastors of the superchurches
approve of these practices, but that they choose not to
"turn off" people who they believe have turned their
backs on Christianity because of such a "legalistic"
emphasis.

The liberal preaching that usually stands at the dia-
metrically opposite end of the theological/social spec-

trum from Fundamentalism also is avoided. Do not expect to hear exhortations on the virtue of economic sanctions in South Africa or on the evils of capitalistic exploitation in the Third World. Nor will there be sermons that deal with such topics as "The Sexist Language of the Apostle Paul" or "The Validity of Alternative Life-Styles." The social values articulated from the pulpits of superchurches will seldom, if ever, contradict the values of middle America. It is not so much that these sermons embody the ideology of the American business community, or express a "yuppified" version of the gospel, but rather that anything that might offend those who hold to such an ideology or embrace such a life-style is carefully omitted.

The sermons of the superchurches deal with the kinds of themes that enable individuals to find peace of mind, and give guidance in dealing with depression and disappointment, help in turning personal failures into personal triumphs, and direction in living more "successful" lives.

Here are some titles of sermons actually preached in one of the more prominent superchurches in America. These examples were chosen randomly and will provide a fairly good idea of what you will hear on Sunday mornings in these houses of worship.

"High on Happiness"

"Hey America—Let's Get Going!"

"How You Can Have the Power to Cope"

"You Can Rise Above Your Circumstances"

"Ego Power and Eagle Power"

"Eagle Power—That Soaring Spirit Can
  Be Yours"

Just about everything that goes on at superchurches is
upbeat. The Sunday morning worship services are
designed to be emphatically entertaining. The music is
contemporary and polished. Band instruments rather
that traditional organs play a new brand of Christian
music that has a rhythm all its own. The old hymns that
are so much a part of traditional Protestantism are heard
only rarely. Of course there will be exceptions. But for
the most part this is the usual fare for those who go to
superchurches.

Bruce Barton and the Man Nobody Knows

The version of Christianity that is presented by the
superchurches is not particularly new. More than fifty
years ago, Bruce Barton, an American advertising agent
straight from Madison Avenue, gave expression to this
kind of religion in a fascinating best-selling book entitled
*The Man Nobody Knows.** Barton's thesis was that Jesus
was able to start the most successful movement in world
history because He preached a message and used techniques that the best experts in the modern advertising
profession are only now beginning to put into practice.
Barton suggests that Jesus was a master of applied psy-
chology who, two thousand years ago, anticipated all
that Dale Carnegie would teach us about winning
friends and influencing people.

---

* Bruce Barton, *The Man Nobody Knows*, New York: Bobbs-Merrill, 1925.

"Jesus had a charming personality," said Barton. He claimed Jesus knew how to "sell" His product, and if He were alive in the flesh today, He undoubtedly would use television to get His message out as extensively as possible. According to Barton, Jesus was the ultimate sales manager and motivator. It was Barton's conviction that He came to teach us the principles for being successful and dynamic people. Barton's Jesus is the incarnation of all the social values of a consumer-oriented society.

Churches for a Television Audience

Another of the obvious reasons for the success of superchurches is that they appeal to people who have been socialized by television. There is little doubt that those who watch TV as much as we Americans do will find the old-fashioned worship so typical of mainline churches uninteresting and even boring. Television has trained us to expect everything to be presented to us in a highly entertaining fashion. We are now a people geared for amusing performances by anybody who wants to communicate with us. We have become accustomed to shows that feature special effects.

The pastors of superchurches are more than aware of this reality. The worship services of superchurches are as entertaining and exciting as most TV shows. It is not surprising that many of them have actually *become* television shows.

One superchurch I know brilliantly employs drama in its Sunday services. Special skits depict the theme of the morning sermon, "setting up" the preacher. These skits demonstrate situations in everyday life with which those in the congregation can readily identify and raise questions about how Christians should handle those situations. The dramatic presentations raise the questions that the preacher endeavors to answer in his morning message. The skits are professionally done and usually humorous. They are just the sort of thing that those in the congregation have grown used to enjoying in shows like the Carol Burnett Show.

The fastest-growing congregation in the Pittsburgh area makes effective use of audiovisual techniques to both entertain and inspire its parishioners. This church has taken hymn singing and turned it into a multimedia presentation. The words of each hymn are flashed up on a huge central screen. (Hymn books are seldom, if ever, used in superchurches.) On each of the viewing screens set on either side of the main central screen, there are flashed in rapid succession an array of slides of scenes related to the messages of the hymns. If a hymn is about the glories of God's creation, glorious pictures of mountains, flowers, and cloud formations are thrown up on the screen in rapid succession. If a hymn is about how God visits us in our loneliness, then the slide pictures on the panel side screens show teenagers, adults, and the elderly in lonely postures with sad expressions on their faces.

To illustrate the content of one of the favorite songs of this congregation, "How Great Thou Art," here are some of the images that were employed:

> Oh Lord my God when I in awesome wonder,
> consider all the worlds Thy hands have made,
> (slides depicting stars, galaxies, and spiral nebulas)

I see the stars, I hear the rolling thunder
Thy power throughout the universe displayed,
(slides depicting lightning flashes and volcanic
eruptions)

The song went on and so did the presentation of a succession of visual images. The efforts were inspiring. The
beauty of the pictures coupled with the message of this
moving song had me almost in tears.

A common device employed in superchurches is the
personal interview with some prominent athlete or film
star. Picking up on the well-developed model made popular by the Johnny Carson Show, a celebrity is brought
on stage during the morning service and enters into an
informal conversation with the pastor. Such interviews
are not limited to athletes and show business stars:
prominent people from all walks of life are used. Astro-
nauts, politicians, famous business figures, and other
easily recognized personalities are all possibilities for
this role. In each case those in the congregation or in the
TV viewing audience find out in an entertaining fashion
how faith has played a crucial role in overcoming problems and in achieving success.

The sermons of superchurch preachers are often mas-
terpieces of oratory. These preachers are often referred to
as "communicators," and they richly deserve the title.
Using an array of illustrations from real life that alter-
nately have their congregations laughing and teary-eyed,
these preachers masterfully hold their congregations in
the palms of their hands. The sermons are always relevant to the personal problems that the listeners face in
their everyday lives, and the preachers always come

across as "real life" persons who themselves are struggling with the same problems. The sermon is not likely to go beyond fifteen or twenty minutes in length, because these preachers know the attention span of a people reared on television. Everyone goes away having been "picked up" by the events of the hour.

Do not get the idea that these preachers give superficial sermons or that they do not meet some deep needs that are a part of human existence. The reverse is true. It is just that these preachers are not social prophets who, like Moses, Jeremiah, or Isaiah, speak out for the oppressed or call down God's judgment on a society that has become secularized into a consumer-oriented lifestyle. Their sermons do speak to personal, individualistic concerns, and almost every one of them does so in a tour de force of homiletical skill.

Most of the ordinary churches with ordinary preachers cannot keep up with either the showmanship or the extensive programs of the superchurches. Consequently, there is a continual leakage of membership from ordinary churches to the superchurches. Ordinary churches just cannot compete.

The superchurches will not call America away from its consumer-oriented ways. And they will not provide a new vision of what we ought to be. In short, they will not be prophetic. But they will be successful and helpful. And they certainly will be entertaining.

Middle-Range Ways in a Great Big Church

In spite of all the negative things that prophets would heap upon superchurches, I think that these churches are beginning to do some things that could change them significantly. I am referring to the fact that, in many of them, people are becoming involved in middle-range efforts to affect the world for Christ. For instance, in Hollywood, California, just off the famous corner of Hollywood and Vine, one of these superchurches has established a ministry to teenage runaways, prostitutes, and street people.

A few young adults from the church have moved into a house that they open up to the hurting people who hang out at this world-famous corner. They provide counseling, temporary housing, and prayer. These dedicated young people are just a handful of a huge congregation, but I think they have a chance of being a sector that could begin to stir the rest of the church to a new vision of what the church should be about.

In Newport Beach, the youth program of a superchurch involves getting teenagers to work in ministries in the slums of Tijuana and in the island nation of Haiti. It may not seem like much in the grand scheme of the multiplicity of programs sponsored by this particular superchurch, but it could sensitize the young people and help to break the false consciousness that characterizes people in this consumer-oriented society.

In Atlanta, Georgia, there is a superchurch that has a good number of its men working regularly with Habitat for Humanity. The impact of this involvement is beginning to show its effects in the overall life of the church. One of the men in this program told me that his work with Habitat was as significant as his "born again" experience when he first came to know about the salvation of Christ. "My work with Habitat has got me on fire," he told me. "Being a Christian has a whole new meaning to me now."

Such instances may not seem to amount to much when we see how few of the people in these churches are involved in them and how little of the money in the multimillion-dollar budgets of those churches is involved. But remember, the Kingdom of God is a Mustard Seed Conspiracy. There's no telling what God can do through such small beginnings. Something as old as the new life preached by the prophets may, through these middle-range efforts, become a transforming influence on a lot of people in the new superchurches that are being born across America.

CHAPTER 8

MAKING IT HAPPEN ON BROAD STREET

Nᴏʀᴛʜ Pʜɪʟᴀᴅᴇʟᴘʜɪᴀ contains one of the worst black ghettos in America. Hundreds of thousands of people live in dilapidated houses owned by landlords. Violent crime is commonplace, as drug cartels compete to control the lucrative trade in "crack" and "ice." Most people are afraid to venture out after dark, and the police who walk the streets are filled with fear. During the daytime hours, children play on vacant lots strewn with trash and junked cars. Teenagers cutting school seem omnipresent. Unemployment in this rundown area is hard to figure; estimates run as high as 40 percent. Storekeepers are closing their businesses because they have been robbed too often and no longer want a daily existence that is fraught with the fear of death.

But in the midst of this dying ghetto, something incredible is happening. A Pentecostal church is growing

by leaps and bounds. This church is committed to doing
what many might consider impossible—rebuilding the
community. Having begun as a storefront church, Deliverance Tabernacle on North Broad Street has steadily
and dramatically increased its membership and now
holds services in what previously had been one of
Philadelphia's largest movie houses. Thousands squeeze
into the Sunday morning services to participate in exu-
berant worship. Emotions are released and ecstasy
expressed in ways that represent the best of the African-
American experience.

The excitement of Deliverance Tabernacle does not
end with Sunday morning worship. In reality, what happens on Sunday is only a launching pad for a variety of
social programs that are earning an impressive list of
successes in the North Philadelphia area. Not only does
this church provide an array of helping services such as
legal counseling, medical care, and recreational programs, but it has embarked on an ambitious plan to
redevelop the living conditions and the economy of the
surrounding neighborhood.

Deliverance Tabernacle has organized and trained
young people to rehabilitate deserted houses, which in
that part of the city number in the thousands. Through
this program, not only are jobs being created for a lot of
teenagers, but inexpensive housing is being offered for
sale to many poor people. The church provides a "total
care" program that involves housing, feeding, and caring
for elderly people in the community, many of whom
previously had lived alone in dingy rat-infested flats.

The most impressive venture of Deliverance has been
its success in developing a new shopping center, complete with a supermarket, a bank, and a variety of small

businesses, including a fast-food outlet. In this shopping center, young men and women are learning how to be retail clerks. Unemployed residents of the area are finding work, and people from blocks around are discovering a good place to shop. Previously, the disintegration of the neighborhood had made such opportunities and services increasingly rare. But with the daring and hard work of the members of Deliverance Tabernacle, this trend has been reversed. The shopping center is doing what many thought could not be done. It is rejuvenating the area. It is creating new life where there had been only social stagnation. Deliverance Tabernacle is initiating what Hebraic scholars call "Shalom" and what Christian theologians call the "Kingdom of God."

Experts in city renewal come from all over the country to see what this church is pulling off. But what has happened under the auspices of Deliverance Tabernacle can hardly be replicated by governments on the city or state levels. This began as a grassroots operation and has been generated out of small groups of people who not only learned to work together but also learned how to pray together.

The ministry of Deliverance Tabernacle is wholly related to the beliefs and practices of its congregation. Every program has been undergirded with prayer. Every administrator has come to his or her position with a sense of having been "called" and ordained by God. All the important decisions that have gone into making these projects successful have been the subjects of long prayer meetings by the people. In so many ways, what has been happening in North Philadelphia through the people of Deliverance Tabernacle is the work of the Holy Spirit.

Deliverance Tabernacle's membership is large enough for it to be considered a superchurch. But it breaks the patterns of most superchurches in that it understands that part of its mission is to change the world and not just to help troubled people to live successful lives in the world that is. Undoubtedly, the mission of Deliverance Tabernacle, in part, comes out of its people. As African-Americans, the members of Deliverance Tabernacle have endured humiliation and oppression from the dominant middle-class white society. They know that such a society must be changed and that they themselves must be a countercultural force helping to make that happen.

Middle-Range Projects Affect the Life of the Church

The reason for focusing on the work of Deliverance Tabernacle is not simply to tell about another grassroots effort to effect social change. What I want to talk about is what has happened to the people of Deliverance Tabernacle in the process of engaging in these social ministries. While what these people have been doing is a blessing to the neighborhood, what I want you to see is that their activities have had an incredible influence on what has been going on in their own personal lives and in the life of their church. The benefits that these projects have reaped for the church people who have brought them about are more than worth the cost that the church has had to pay in carrying them out. They have given to the people of Deliverance a whole new quality of spirituality.

First of all, there is the effect that this outreach has had on the young people of the church. As they have organized to carry out various responsibilities connected with these projects, they have developed an intense closeness. They have become best friends. From the beginning, these young people have spent most of their spare time together. They have become, in the words of sociologist Charles Cooley, a "primary group." Their intense relationships have served to reinforce the Christian values they had learned at church and have helped to give them clear personal identities.

Living as they do, in a social environment that is both anti-Christian and delinquent, it is nearly impossible for most teenagers and young adults in an area like this to stand alone and to withstand the pressures to conform. But with the constant reinforcing of Christian values and the regular revitalization of the identity that has come from participation in their youth group at Deliverance Tabernacle, these young people have gained the wherewithal to stand firm. The relationships developed in social action through the church have given them the fortitude and courage to maintain a Christian counterculture mentality in the midst of a very tough environment. Were this not the case, the dominant society would probably have swallowed them up and enculturated them into its own image. Instead, these primary groups, formed to carry out assignments related to the church's neighborhood development projects, have made these young people more than able to survive as a "peculiar people" (I Pet. 2:9).

All of this only heightens our awareness of the need to create small groups of Christians who will work together to do the work of the Kingdom. Such groups create what biblical scholars call *koinonia*, a special kind of fellowship that belongs to those who feel spiritual oneness in Christ.

Groups that get together simply to ensure their own survival rarely last. But when a group has a mission that carries it beyond its own self-interest, its members usually find that their common mission cements them together. More important, we should note that it is only in the context of such intensely committed groups that a countercultural value system can be maintained and a clear understanding of what it means to be a radical Christian established.

Peter Berger, one of America's most popular contemporary sociologists, gives a great deal of attention to this process of identity reinforcement within a primary group. Berger contends that, in order to maintain a consciousness that is other than that prescribed by the dominant society, the individual must be part of what he calls a "plausibility structure." This is a small group that serves to keep individuals from coming to think that they are crazy or that their beliefs are unreal. According to Berger, the only way that a person can go on believing that a countercultural belief system is viable is by having it regularly revitalized within a plausibility structure that shares that belief system.

A Way to Be Filled with the Spirit

Evangelical Christians, particularly of the Charismatic stripe, have come to discover some supernatural benefits from such small-group relationships. These benefits far transcend what sociologists can observe empirically. Christians are discovering that in small groups that are committed to Christian mission, there is often a mystical encounter with the power and presence of the Holy Spirit. While I am not attempting here to spell out the whys and wherefores of how the Holy Spirit works in the world, I am suggesting that the most "normal" way to experience the Spirit is in the context of small-group relationships. I believe that this is what Jesus was getting at when He said, "For where two or three are gathered together in my name, there am I in the midst of them" (Matt. 18:20). I believe that somehow the Holy Spirit chooses to emerge in a special way when small groups of Christians interact meaningfully and intensely. I believe that the Holy Spirit comes *through* the others to the individual and *through* the individual to the others.

Jesus Himself had such a support group. It was composed of Peter, James, and John. Whenever there were to be high times of spiritual ecstasy, such as on the Mount of Transfiguration (Mark 9:2–12), these three were chosen to be with Him. He loved the twelve, but these three were special. He took them away from the others to pray with great regularity.

As the Son of Man, as Jesus liked to call Himself, He was in *need* of the renewal of the Spirit that could come in the context of the intense prayer and fellowship that He shared with His small company of disciples. That, of course, is what made Gethsemane so painful for Him. It appears that in the hour when He most needed the spiritual revitalization that comes from such mutual intimacy in the Spirit, His support group fell asleep on Him, leaving Him to struggle with His painful destiny alone.

What Jesus sought in His small prayer group is, in a limited way, what the young people of Deliverance Tabernacle found in their small groups. And, from a sociological perspective, that small-group experience is the primary means for maintaining a life-style of non-conformity in a world in which being a Christian is often countercultural. At a time in American Christianity when people want to *experience* God, not just believe in Him, such small-group encounters become increasingly important to the Christian life-style that is meaningful to them.

Serving As Though People Matter

So often, social programs designed by government agencies fail to take the people being served into consideration. Those who come up with grand schemes for society often overlook the concerns of individuals. Macro programs are usually carried out by "experts" who assume they know what people need more than the people themselves do. Certainly this was the case when, in the late fifties and early sixties, the government attempted to address the need for low-cost housing in America. Architects, social workers, and government officials were involved in the planning and building of high-rise buildings to house poor people who, for the most part, were on public assistance (i.e., welfare).*

Nobody asked the people who would have to live in these units what they wanted. Consequently, when these buildings were erected, they proved to be dysfunctional. Children out playing were not about to take an elevator up twenty floors to go to the toilet. The way in which the buildings were constructed kept neighbors from getting

---

*See Jane Jacobs, *Death and Life of the Great American Cities*, New York: Random House, 1961.

to know each other, and the hallways of many of these buildings proved to be unsafe late at night.

There are a host of other examples of how urban planners and government social workers, for all of their good intentions, often fail in their efforts simply because they do not listen to the people whom they are trying to serve.

The opposite was true of those who developed the social ministries of Deliverance Tabernacle. The Deliverance projects have been carried out by people who knew the residents of the community. Actually, most of them were residents of the area and talked constantly to their neighbors about the things that their church was trying to do. Small grassroots groups have a sensitivity to neighborhood sentiments that macro planners can never have. That is why projects designed and executed by small groups of people working on the community level are far more effective than those that are planned and carried out by women and men who sit in offices of power at city hall or in Washington.

As Deliverance Tabernacle members carried out their church's plans for community development, many of them learned new ways to relate effectively to their neighbors and community leaders. As individuals they developed self-confidence. They overcame the reluctance that sometimes keeps people from confrontations over points of difference. They learned how to develop a community consensus on difficult issues.

A side effect that few people expected when these social service projects were first initiated was a significant evangelistic outreach for the church. The discussions with neighbors about what the church was doing and the possible consequences of these efforts on the community opened the doors for discussion about Christ and what He wills for the world. Many who at first were only interested in what the projects would do for or to the community were soon involved in deep spiritual discussions about Christ and the Kingdom of God. Several who wanted to participate in making the neighborhood a more decent place in which to live were soon drawn into the life of the church and into a personal commitment to the Gospel.

Additionally, the various projects of Deliverance Tabernacle gave new meaning to the prayer life of the church. Elderly shut-ins now spend long hours praying for those in positions of leadership and asking for divine intervention as difficult barriers and problems arise. Weekly midweek prayer meetings at church are now well attended as people of the church come to lean on Jesus for help and guidance. Participants in these projects sense that the work they have to do is too much for them to handle alone, and they have learned to go to the Lord in prayer. The vitality of the prayer life of Deliverance Tabernacle has increased dramatically as a result of the church's community involvement through its people.

I tell the story of Deliverance Tabernacle because I believe that the things this church is doing and the ways in which its people are being changed are examples of what has to happen all across the land if America is to be saved. I believe that if people in cities, towns, and villages throughout America would be mobilized into community-based efforts to solve pressing problems and to meet human needs, then there could be a new beginning for our people.

Praxis Lived Out

Sociologists use the term *praxis* to refer to the belief that people are changed by what they do. But they do not mean pure activism when they talk of praxis. They are referring to something far deeper. Praxis is action in reflection and/or reflection in action. It is a special kind of thinking that takes place when people are actually doing things. People do one kind of thinking when they read or discuss ideas. They do another kind of thinking when they are involved in trying to change the world. The first kind of thinking is the prerogative of scholars. The second takes place in the minds of those who are caught up in an intense struggle to solve the problems that are part of their everyday lives as they try to earn a living, raise a family, fight crime in their community, and make their schools responsive to the needs of their children. The first kind of thinking creates opinions that can be changed. The second kind forms convictions that change those who think that way.

What has been going on at Deliverance Tabernacle has been praxis. People are not just doing things; they are being changed by what they do. The false consciousness perpetrated by their consumer-oriented society is being broken, and they are seeing the world in a new light. Their struggles in trying to carry out their middle-range programs for social change have gotten them into a new frame of mind. What is important to them, how they view themselves, and what they think their lives are all about have all changed. God is doing a new thing among them. They are coming alive. They are people with a new vision. They are a people filled with new dreams.

I have talked to them. I have watched the eyes of their youth flash with excitement. I have seen older people demonstrate the energy of fleet-footed deer. I have seen what prophets have always hoped would happen to people actually taking place in these small beginnings.

It is embryonic. It is small. It is like a mustard seed. But there is new life there. There is something that could be a foretaste of a new America.

A Theory of Social Change

Many would go along with my claims that the middle-range activities of the people at Deliverance Tabernacle have done them a lot of good. But skeptics and doomsayers would go on to say that, while such things can get people "feeling good," the social system itself will remain unchanged.

"You don't really think that such middle-range projects are going to change the social structures of this country, do you?" they would ask. "You don't really believe all of that George Bush stuff about a thousand points of light?"

Of course I do. And I'm not the only one. A lot of brilliant sociologists would back me up and say the same thing.

Alexis de Tocqueville saw that such local, community-based ventures were what made America work. Back in the early nineteenth century, de Tocqueville made it clear that the diffusion of democracy in a thousand town meetings for the planning and creating of schools, hospitals, and fire companies was what made America's people alive and dynamic. More contemporary social scientists like Robert Nisbet, Peter Berger, and Talcott Parsons would say the same thing. *Small is Beautiful* could be more than a title of a book. It could easily be the slogan for this style of social change, which I believe could bring new hope and life to the American people.

If the last couple of decades have taught us anything, they should have taught us that trying to change the structure of society from the top down does not work very well. During the Reagan years there was much talk about supply-side economics and trickle-down economic theory. The word coming out of Washington then was an up-to-date version of the old line, "What's good for General Motors is good for the country." In more direct terms, all that meant was that if big business was thriving it would stimulate the development and growth of smaller businesses, and new jobs would be created throughout the social system. The idea was that the smaller businesses have the bigger businesses as customers, so the health of the latter should determine the health of the former.

In many ways the Reagan years provided some startling economic successes. By the end of President Reagan's eight years in office, America had recovered from an economic slump, and more Americans were gainfully employed than at any other time in history. Republicans were delirious with the success of the Reagan Administration, and Democrats were wondering how, if ever, they could retake the White House.

But were things as they seemed? Had big business really saved America? Did the tax breaks and incentives that government provided for the heavy industries and the big corporations really do the job?

Actually, the answer has proven to be "No!" While big business provided some stimulation for the development of small businesses, the truth is that things were the other way around. Small businesses were what got big business and big industry rolling.

Any analysis of the economic scene during the Reagan years would demonstrate that what really happened was that small entrepreneurs provided the primary job-creating force in America. From one end of this country to the other, small businesses and small industries created by a host of enterprising risk takers were the ones who really put Americans back to work in record numbers. The people employed by these small businesses and industries had money to spend, and they bought things. And it is when they began buying the likes of automobiles, television sets, refrigerators, and stoves that the big industries that produced them started doing well. Positive social change occurs on the micro level first. It is there that the forces that make the economy go are unleashed.

This lesson is not going unnoticed in Third World countries. One by one the poor nations of the world are beginning to abandon their schemes for massive, planned economic development and are concentrating on encouraging the development of small cottage industries and small businesses. Operations that involve ten or fifteen people are much more likely to succeed than are massive industries that are, in theory, supposed to create jobs for hundreds or even thousands of workers.

Small businesses, it has been learned, create new jobs at a much lower cost than do large industries. For instance, in a high-tech big business, it may take as much as $100,000 to create a single employment opportunity. A small business can create a new job for as little as $100.

Opportunity International, a Chicago-based Christian missionary organization, grasped this fact and has set up a job creation program based on it. It has concentrated on providing loans to Third World entrepreneurs who demonstrate a capacity to start small businesses or cottage industries. The results of Opportunity International have been amazing. Working in forty-six countries, with limited funds, Opportunity International has generated more than thirty-six thousand jobs. It has led the way for a whole new kind of missionary work. Young men and women are regularly signing up to work with this organization, because they are convinced that, by creating these "intermediate units" in Third World economies, they can be the most effective kinds of agents of social change.

At Eastern College, where we have a graduate program designed to prepare missionaries to do this kind of development work, I have an easy time convincing students that they are the real hope for the future. I tell them something like this:

> You could go into a small city like Cap Haitien, Haiti, and over a decade create forty or sixty small businesses. Assuming that each of these businesses ends up employing ten people, you could be supplying jobs for as many as six hundred families in that city. Knowing, as you do, that people who earn money spend money, you can surmise that the working people who spend what they earn will create still more jobs.

How long do you think that it will be before there is a good educational system in that city? If people have money to pay teachers, don't you think that there will be a decent school fairly soon?

How long do you think it will take to get good medical services there? If people can pay for doctors, don't you think that there will be not only doctors, but hospitals and clinics as well?

How long do you think it will be before there is an adequate food supply in that city? When there is money to buy food, how long do you think it will take before the food is available?

In the end, how long will it be before a democratic political system is called for? If wealth is distributed in an egalitarian fashion through job creation, how long do you think it will take before there will be a government that is responsive to the needs of the people?

Of course, things never work out as simply as my speech suggests. But there is enough truth to the plan to make the students believe that they can make a difference in the macro scheme of things by creating middle-range economic units.

Small Is Beautiful in Education, Too

In the fifties and sixties, there was a big drive to consolidate educational systems. Local school districts were obliterated as regional school systems took their places. Consolidation was so popular that there were some who were talking about a national school system run out of Washington.

Well, things have turned around. In Chicago, they are now experimenting with attempts to break down the school system into small community units. There is the conviction that the citywide school system is too cumbersome to be effective and that its massive nature has left people feeling powerless to influence what goes on in the educational lives of their children. So now local communities are being allowed to elect their own boards of education, which in turn will be responsible for what goes on in the local schools. The people in the community will be able to have direct access to the decision-making processes that determine who gets hired and what gets taught. Their children will no longer be out of their control. Across America, large municipalities are waiting to see how this experiment with middle-range educational units works.

The Church As Initiator

Middle-range activity, as a means of recreating America and giving new life to its people, is more and more being seen as a redeeming force in this country. But we all know that for anything to start on the local level there has to be a catalyst. There has to be some agency or person from whom comes initiative, inspiration, and vision. *Enter the church!* I am convinced that the church can play this crucial role. I believe that the church was *meant* to play this role. I believe that it was for such a mission that the church was created in the first place. The church has the value system that can provide the basis for altruistic service. Sometimes the church has lost sight of its biblical imperatives to be a "suffering servant" for the world and has become as self-interested and self-contained as any of the worldly institutions that surround it. But the Bible is always there to tell the church what it is supposed to be and do. And more often than its critics are ready to admit, pastors and preachers call the church back to its high calling.

The church has all that is needed to make middle-range programs happen. In its laity are the human resources to organize community projects and the skills to translate dreams and visions into concrete reality. The church also has the financial resources that are needed for these ventures.

Frequently, the clergy has refused to release church lay persons for ministry outside the immediate interests of the institutional church. And more often than those of us in the church want to admit, the church leaders have kept its wealth to serve only ecclesiastical interests. But there are prophetic voices within the church that are calling its people to give themselves and all they own away to meet the needs of a needy world. There are Mother Teresa and Bishop Tutu, as well as countless hundreds of others who have not won Nobel prizes, who call for such sacrifices. And their voices *are* being heard.

The church has the vision that is needed for the rebirth of America. That vision is a new humanity, which has been revealed in Jesus Christ. It is the dream of a new society filled with loving responsibility. That vision has been fleshed out in the life of the Christians portrayed in the book of Acts. All that has to happen is for the church to be The Church and America will have what it needs to live again.

A Parable for the Church

There was a land where there was a great oil refinery. The refinery was gigantic and was known to employ all the modern techniques of chemical engineering. Its facilities were bright and shining, and those who worked there made sure that everything was kept in good condition and that everything ran well.

One day, some visitors to the land asked to have a tour of the refinery. At first there was reluctance to show the visitors what they wanted to see. But when the visitors insisted, the rulers of the land directed that they be given an extensive tour of the refinery.

After seeing the vast chambers for processing petroleum, the gleaming pipes that carried the petroleum products from place to place, and the extensive organizational system that had been set in place to keep the refinery going, the visitors asked to see the shipping department. "What shipping department?" asked the tour guide in response.

"Why, the shipping department from whence you ship out all the gasoline and oil that you process here," said the tourists.

"We don't have any shipping department," answered the guide. "You see, all the energy products produced in this refinery are used up keeping the refinery going."

Sometimes I think that the church is as absurd as that make-believe refinery. At times it functions in much the same way. I would have to join the critics who say that most of the energy that the church produces is used up for nothing more than keeping the church going. Its money and its people are in large measure used up to maintain the institution, and relatively little goes out to meet the needs of the world. That has to change.

At its best, the church is the only organization that exists solely for the good of its nonmembers. At its best, the church understands the words of Christ and knows that if it seeks to save itself, it will lose itself, but if it is willing to give itself away to meet the needs of others, it will live. The church must live up to its calling. A dying nation and a people who have lost their collective soul are depending on it.

In concrete terms, America waits for one hundred thousand churches to give away their human and financial resources to build houses for the poor and shelters for street people; organize crusades to save the environment; create jobs for the unemployed; provide help to single mothers, decent education for the socially disinherited, and deliverance for those who are being dehumanized in prison; and do a hundred and one other things that need to be done on the local level by community people. To respond to these needs, churches will have to preach the gospel to win converts as never before. But these new converts will not be people who "get saved" just so that they can go to heaven. Instead, they will be a people of God, committed to be agents of God's revolution. They will be part of the Mustard Seed Conspiracy composed of middle-range efforts carried out by a people who are coming to life.

CHAPTER 9

GETTING DOWN WHERE IT COUNTS

IT ALL DEPENDS ON THE preachers—those men and women who occupy pulpits and pastor the thousands of "ordinary" churches across America. They are the ones who really hold our destiny in their hands. If people are going to be challenged to new life, if they are going to be drawn together to change things for God, if all of those middle-range efforts I have been talking about and the personal transformations that occur in praxis are to happen, then the preachers must live up to their calling. According to St. Paul,

How then shall they call on him in whom they have not believed? and how shall they believe in him of whom they have not heard? and how shall they to hear without a preacher? (Rom. 10:14)

There is no doubt that if the spiritual renewal for which
the prophets seek ever takes place in America, it will be
because the "ordinary" preachers in "ordinary" churches do extraordinary things.

The revival will not come from the superchurches. As
good as they are at healing the wounds of a battered generation, they do not make the prophetic mission the primary focus of their ministries. As large as they are, they
do not reach enough people to turn around a nation.
Most Americans still go to "ordinary" churches, and it
is in them that the miracle of the rebirth of mission
must begin.

Neither will the revival come from those small countercultural churches that follow the lead of the Sojourners Community. Though the prophetic message that
they proclaim is at the heart of what the biblical message is all about, they lack the touch with the masses
that is essential for stirring us to a new vision and a new
future.

It is to the leaders of "ordinary" churches that we
must look. They must stir us, if not to radical commitment, at least to be a people who understand the message of Christ clearly enough to call into question how
we have been living. They must lead us, if not into a revolutionary countercultural course of action, at least to
engage in a host of middle-range projects that reflect the
Kingdom of God. If they fail, we fail. If they fail, we have
a right to be angry with them.

Jesus and the lesser prophets of scripture were hard on
the religious leaders of their times, not because they hated them, but because they were so disappointed in
them. Those who lead the people of God at worship and

head up the ministry of God's people in the world have an incredible responsibility to preach and teach the things that make for revival. And when they fail, the prophets are always angry. James the Apostle warns that those who teach the word of God will be held more accountable for what happens to people than anyone else (James 3:1). We need a revival in the land, but we must recognize that such a revival must be led by those who have been ordained by "ordinary" churches to lead the people in the things of the spirit.

Concerts of Prayer for Preachers

The validity of what I am saying must be apparent. And yet it sends slight tremors up and down our spines. We hate to admit it, but those who lead our churches do not inspire us with confidence. Some seem beaten down because of constant criticism and picking that usually comes from members and elders in their churches. Some seem paralyzed with the fear of losing the status and income that goes with their jobs. Some, overcome by disillusion, have given up on their dreams and settled down to the routines of running an institution. Some have simply lost their "first love" and are spiritually cold (Rev. 2:4). And some are just plain tired.

We need not just sit back, throw up our hands, and resign ourselves to the sorry condition of these discouraged men and women who have been called to lead us. *We can pray.*

I suppose that you knew I was going to say that. You may even be thinking that this kind of statement is the sort of cop-out to be expected from somebody who doesn't know what else to say and who has no *practical* suggestions to make. Nothing could be farther from the truth.

In the Bible, prophets arose because the people prayed for God to raise them up. When the children of Israel felt that they were living in a spiritual wasteland, they prayed that God would give them a prophet, and God answered their prayers. In Bible days, the revival of a people and the renewal of the nation always began with prayer. Without prayer there were no prophets.

We do not pay enough attention to how prayer works. Through prayer, God channels His power *through* people *to* people. By that I mean that, through prayer, I can do more than make requests known to God. It is also possible through prayer to make myself available to God to be a conduit through whom His Spirit can flow toward another person. In prayer I can open myself up to be filled with the power of God. Then I can mentally and spiritually direct all of that power toward some person or persons and become a lens through which the light and power of God can be focused onto the lives of others. When I do that, I can sense that God is using me as a means through whom His dynamistic Spirit goes out into the world to affect lives and make miracles happen.

The Strange Experiences of Frank Laubach

Frank Laubach, the famous missionary and educator, tells of going into a church on an Easter Sunday morning and finding it a spiritually deadening experience. Instead of accepting things as they were, he decided to be spiritually aggressive. He decided to go at the pastor and the members of the congregation in the power of the Holy Spirit.

First Laubach decided to work on the pastor. He tells how he surrendered himself to the infilling of the Spirit and then directed what he was receiving from God at the man in the pulpit. The effects, said Laubach, were almost immediate and also more than apparent. That preacher's message gradually began to evidence life and vitality. The words of the sermon came alive, and the pastor's entire being seemed to throb with excitement.

Then, according to Laubach, the individuals in the congregation became the subjects of his empowering prayers. One by one, he picked out persons in the congregation and focused the enlivening power of God toward each of them. The results, he contends, were amazing. He tells how he actually saw heads jerk back as he focused on them. It seemed that the Spirit flowing through him was awakening each of them to hear the gospel. The congregation became every bit as alive as the pastor. Soon an awesome dynamic filled the place, and a spirit of revival was alive in that church.

When the worship service was over, people were both spiritually alive and puzzled. As Laubach talked to them, they said over and over that something had happened to them in that service that had never happened to them in church before.

On the way out of the church, Frank Laubach talked to the pastor and complimented him on his message. The pastor, who seemed a bit befuddled, said, "I don't understand it. I don't think I ever preached like that before. When I stepped into the pulpit, I felt more spiritually dry than I ever had before. But about five minutes into the sermon, I felt seized by God and I began to preach things that I had never planned to say. And it was wonderful!"

If one man can focus the Spirit on a preacher and res-
urrect him from the dead, can you imagine what would
happen if a whole group of people joined together and
gave themselves to that task? Can you imagine what
could happen if all across this country groups of church
members not only prayed *for* their pastors, but became
channels through whom the Holy Spirit could flow
toward pastors? Might not these pastors be empowered
to be prophets? Might not revival begin in the house-
holds of God? Might this not be the beginning of the
spiritual renewal that American needs?

To the laity of America's churches, I make this plea.
Would each of you ask some others in your church who
crave revival to covenant with you to pray *for* your pastors, and would you commit yourselves to becoming
channels through whom the Holy Spirit can empower
them?

Your pastor need not know about it. Tell him or her
about your covenant to pray only if you think that the
knowledge of what is going on would provide encourage-
ment.

I long to hear of countless prayer vigils being held for
pastors. And I can hardly wait to see the consequences of
Christians sitting in congregations on Sunday mornings
focusing the power of the Spirit, like laser beams, upon
those who are preaching the word.

Seminaries That Help Rather Than Hinder

It would help if the seminaries of America trained pastors to do the things that make for revival. They could
start by taking another look or two at what they are

teaching candidates for the Christian ministry. If we are to have the kind of pastoral leadership that can motivate church members into the kinds of middle-range programs that we need to affect communities, and if we are to have the kind of praxis among Christians that will give them a revived spirituality, we need the seminaries to rethink their missions.

When, some thirty-five years ago, I announced to a friend of mine who was the pastor of a large African-American church that I was going to go to seminary, my black friend responded by asking, "What are you doing that for? By the time they finish with you at that place, you won't have enough power to preach the fuzz off a peach!"

There was much truth to that preacher's warning. Seminary did, in many ways, have a stifling effect on my enthusiasm for ministry. The studies in textual criticism, the rationalized theologies, and the courses in church management all had a tendency to socialize me into a religious bureaucrat who was ready to run an institution but was not very certain why he was doing it. What the sociologist Max Weber called the "routinization of charisma" occurs in seminaries and causes some of us to wonder whether or not such institutions are good for the training of preachers. I have seen far too many seminarians lose "something" during their three years of training for me to leave these crucial institutions unscathed by any kind of critique.

In reflection, it may have been what the seminaries did *not* teach me that irritates me more than anything else about them. In talking to others in the Christian ministry, I get a general opinion that their seminaries left them unprepared to be effective in their calling. It is almost as though there were a need for a seminary equivalent of the best-selling book, *What They Didn't Teach Me at Harvard Business School*.

I have talked to a lot of ministers and have had an opportunity to reflect on my own experiences. The following is a list of some of the things that I wished I had learned during my days of ministerial training.

1. *I wish they had told me not to get involved in building programs*. Somehow the clergy are easily seduced into what I call "the edifice complex." I know I certainly was. It is the idea that you are not really succeeding in ministry and your church isn't really progressing unless you put up a new Christian education facility, or better still, a bigger sanctuary for worship.

I have found that all too often, building buildings kills the dynamic of churches and tends to divert the attention of the people from the real mission of Christianity. People often become so preoccupied with building-fund drives and with the color of the new carpeting that they lose sight of their responsibility to minister to the needs of those who are hurting and to communicate the good news of God's love to those who need to be saved. I am sure that there are exceptions, but in more cases than not, building programs use up a lot of money and energy that would better be used in outreach ministries to those in the outside world.

In America we have spent over $180 billion on church buildings to honor one who told us, "I dwell not in temples made with human hands." Think of what might have happened, not only to America but to the people in

America's churches, if that money, and the energy that goes with it, had been spent on the following:

- Building houses for the poor
- Sponsoring ministries for runaway teenagers
- Providing shelters for the homeless
- Setting up care centers for those with drug addictions
- Establishing halfway houses for prison inmates
- Carrying out local efforts to clean up the environment
- Providing medical and legal services for poor people
- Creating small businesses to provide employment for jobless people
- Setting up latchkey and tutoring programs for socially disadvantaged children
- Providing help and services for single parents
- Undergirding efforts in minority communities to overcome the effects of racism and poverty
- Setting up care centers for battered women
- Developing both total care and day care for the elderly
- Developing AIDS hospices
- Providing counseling and an education fund for potential college students who come from poor backgrounds
- Creating service ministries on Native American reservations
- Financing Christian art

The list could go on and on. But more important than any and all of these is the question of what would have happened if that money and effort had been channeled into the kind of holistic evangelism that makes Jesus Christ real and meaningful to millions who only know about Him.

I am not suggesting that there is never a need for new buildings and Christian education facilities. But in most instances there are alternatives. The movie theater in town could be used for Sunday morning services; so could the banquet hall at the local Holiday Inn or Sheraton hotel. There are schools that can be rented on weekends for Sunday School classes, and high school gyms and auditoriums that are available. The idea of spending piles of money for building space that is usually used for only a few hours a week seems like a bad one to me.

In seminary they never taught me about the hidden costs of a building program. They never explained that if I organized my people to put up a sanctuary or a Christian education building, there would be little attention and few resources given to those middle-range programs and projects that can make churches into transforming agents in their communities. They never made it clear that unless the church used its people and its wealth for the latter rather than the former, the church would be seen by those outside it as an institution that wanted to *use* them to pay off mortgages instead of as a group of self-sacrificing people who were responding to the needs of a hurting world.

2. *I wish they had told me that every church I served should really be seen as more than one congregation, and that I should have different ministries for each of them.* In almost every church, first of all, there are the traditionalists. They are the ones who want the church to function only in forms with which they have always been familiar. Inexperienced pastors have a strong tendency to want to shake these "old buzzards" out of their

traditional molds and *make* them experience new styles of worship and new dimensions of Christian mission. As a matter of fact, that is precisely what I came out of seminary thinking I was supposed to do.

If I had it to do over again, I wouldn't be so hard on these traditionalists. If they find worship more meaningful in their time-honored forms, I would respect that and give them the gospel in those old forms. If the established ways of carrying on ministry are the ones that they prefer, I could honor that.

It wouldn't have killed me to have paid a visit to the monthly meeting of the Ladies' Missionary Society. As a matter of fact, I might actually have enjoyed it. And the Annual Strawberry Festival isn't some evil thing that must be set aside for something more "theologically relevant." The Strawberry Festival just might be a good time to relax and visit with people.

That visitation program that the old deacons said would get me into every home of the families of the church each year is really not a bad idea. This is particularly true if the conversation moves beyond the small talk that often characterizes such visits and gets into the real joys and difficulties of living a spiritual life.

However, while I was doing all of these traditional things, I would also nurture another congregation in the church that had another vision of what the church should be and do. And in every church you can find them. These people could worship at an hour that differed from the traditional hour of worship. Their worship service, with all of its banners and contemporary music, might even take place on a Saturday night. Traditionalists can be quite tolerant of alternative forms of worship as long as nobody *forces* them to share in it and if some respect is shown for what they like. The creative kinds of middle-range programs and projects that I have been talking about can usually be started up with few problems as long as I don't disturb what the traditionalists have always been doing. A great deal of innovation can take place without making traditionalists unhappy.

If I didn't have enough of "my own" people for such new approaches to ministry and service, I would work ecumenically. There undoubtedly would be other churches with other pastors who have the same kind of hunger for innovation and daring.

There are three relatively small churches I know about that each week have one shared creative worship service together. The pastors and the people who share in this creative ecumenical worship service chip in to pay the salary of a special minister who leads a youth program involving teenagers from all three of the churches. These pastors are beginning to get people together to build housing for the poor in the community, and they are also developing a shared ministry that is getting their people involved with an inner-city tutoring program. All of this is happening without angering the traditionalists, who only want to worship on Sunday at eleven.

In seminary, I was taught that the ecumenical movement was always some theological thing that was supposed to lead to denominational mergers. They never told me that it was about networking creatively to develop the new kinds of ministries that communities need, and that a lot of people in the churches need if they are going to be alive in Christ.

Of course, when I suggest such things, ministers often cry that they just could never find the time to do all of these creative things and still keep the traditional programs. I can just hear them complaining, "Those middle-range programs that you are talking about are for people with time on their hands. I don't have time to keep up with the things I have got to do now. All this talk about organizing people for community outreach programs ignores my time limitations." That leads me to the third lesson left untaught in seminary.

3. *I wish they had taught me something about time management.* Most of the ministers I know end up immobilized and doing very little in the course of a week. This is primarily because they just do not know how to organize time to get things done.

Many ministers kid others and themselves into believing that they do extensive reading and spend long hours in sermon preparation. Most of them don't. Most sermons are Saturday-night jobs—and it shows.

Ministers claim that they must attend endless meetings. And they may be half right. A good number of those meetings might not really be necessary. Too often, meetings are held for the sake of meeting. And worse than that, often very little planning goes into getting ready for church meetings. An agenda is seldom prepared ahead of time, and a schedule for issues to be discussed is rarely established. The result is that church meetings are usually the longest, dullest meetings any of us ever attend.

Ministers must learn to trust the laity. One reason ministers are so pressed for time is that they feel that they have to do everything themselves. Too often, ministers are on mini–power trips and they are afraid to let anybody else in on the work of their churches for fear that they might have to let go of some of that power. But if ministers in ordinary churches would turn over a lot of what they control to ordinary lay persons, they would have a lot more time to do a lot of extraordinary things.

4. *I wish they had taught me that I ought to spend most of my time in my home town.* It is so easy if you are in a mainline denomination to get sucked into denominational work and end up giving away too much time to what has no bearing on local ministry and the local church. I suppose that denominational meetings are important for those who want to climb up the religious ladder of success. But I have a feeling that most of those who climb that ladder end up realizing when they get to the top that the ladder was leaning against the wrong wall.

I myself have spent huge chunks of time going to denominational meetings that I now know were a waste of time. Long hours were spent hammering out watered-down resolutions that said almost nothing on such issues as abortion, homosexuality, and the Middle East, only to have those resolutions ignored by politicians and sometimes do little more than irritate people in the local congregations.

I fully realize that state and national denominational youth conventions are of great value and that denominational mission work is usually the most progressive in vision and most dollar efficient. But denominational executives know what they are doing, and all of those powwows to get "input" from local pastors is more of an exercise in public relations than a good way of developing programs. A lot of valuable time that is needed on the local level gets wasted.

Ministers must learn to stay put. Local initiatives gain wide support only if community people are convinced that the ministers who are inspiring them to action are there for the long haul. Time and time again I have to listen to young ministers who are just out of seminary complain about the reluctance of their congregations to get moving on any of their grand schemes. "Why should they?" I ask myself. After all, those people are not dummies. They know that the ambitious young preacher with the "big ideas" is going to be moving on to "bigger and better things" in just a short time, leaving them holding the bag. I know because I was once one of those brash young ministers. The fact that churches survive the likes of me is sufficient testimony to the grace of God.

Over the last fifteen years, my co-workers and I have been working with community people in several low-cost government housing projects in the run-down sections of Philadelphia. What my team of workers has pulled off is a justifiable source of the right kind of pride. They have made the kind of middle-range programs that I have been telling you about really work. But the success of the Evangelical Association for the Promotion of Education has been largely due to its staying power.

The first few years we were engaged in ministry, we gained very little community support. We were, at best, tolerated. The people of these communities had seen social workers and community organizers come and go. They had become skeptical about the big talk about the big plans that such people brought with them. When we came along, we were put in the same category as that long line of "do-gooders" who had marched through these people's communities. It took almost five years before they came to trust us. And they did not come to trust us until they were sure we were not going to go away. When we bought houses and moved into the community, they knew we were not carpetbaggers but rather people who wanted to belong. It was then that they accepted us and things began to happen.

During my days in college and seminary, I was fortunate enough to be a student assistant pastor with a senior minister who had his head screwed on right. His name is John David Burton. He is now retired from the full-time pastorate (thought not from service to the Kingdom). That part of his ministry was confined to two communities—Mt. Holly, New Jersey, where I worked with him, and Clarendon Hills, Illinois. When a preacher stays in towns as long as John David did, people learn to support the dreams and visions that are articulated from the pulpit. He showed me the kinds of things that a pastor is able to inspire if he or she stays put.

The other thing that John David taught me was how to use time. I had to be in the office at 8:00 in the morning, and I had to go from there into the community to carry out a list of responsibilities that had been carefully scheduled for me. What I was able to accomplish in Mt. Holly, just working on weekends, astounds me as I look back on those formative years. But I was able to do it because I worked with a man who had been in town long enough to know what had to be done and who made me use my time efficiently in getting it done. He regularly recited to me his favorite line: "The children of darkness are wiser than the children of light—and they work harder too! Let's turn that around."

I am fortunate to have worked with John David Burton. He taught me what I should have learned in seminary. If there were more John David Burtons around, the revival might already be further along.

CHAPTER 10

EVEN TILL THE END OF THIS AGE

As a kid growing up in America, the only reason I could figure out for wanting to be converted was so that I could go to heaven when I died. Since I wasn't planning on dying in the near future, the conversion thing had very little attraction for me. I maintained this indifference to conversion through most of my teenage years. And I did so in spite of the evangelists who visited my church and warned the likes of me that we were in mortal danger.

"You think nothing's going to happen to you because you're young," the evangelists would shout. "Well, you could walk out of this church tonight, be walking across the street, and get hit by a truck. Then where would you be? In Heaven? Or in Hell?"

That sort of threat never really got to me, although I must admit that it did make me more cautious about crossing streets.

But as I grew older, I discovered that something was missing from my life. I am sure you have heard that line before. It is usually the line that those who give their testimonies at religious gatherings can be counted on to give. The line has become a cliché. But like most clichés, it became one because it is true.

Most people reach a time when they become susceptible to what I call "the Peggy Lee syndrome" and say to themselves, "Is this all there is?" Like myself, they begin to look for some ultimate meaning to their lives. So it was that I began to ask why I was here.

Why was I me and not someone else? Was I just an accident, or did my life have some kind of purpose and plan? Questions like those began to haunt me.

My Calvinistic Calling

In my teen years, I came under some solid Calvinistic teachings. The doctrines of John Calvin left me convinced that God had a plan for my life and that being a Christian was not just believing in Jesus and what He had done for me on the cross but also involved committing myself to living out His plan for my life.

I did not have any specifics, but I knew that His plan involved my participation with Him in trying to change the world into the kind of world that He wants it to be. Whether it was preaching to win people to Christ so that they could be people of His Kingdom, teaching in the classroom to prepare young people to be agents of change, or engaging in direct action against the war in Vietnam or to save the environment, I always saw my calling as living out the Lord's Prayer. I always wanted to see the Kingdom come "on earth as it is in heaven."

I want to invite others to share in that commitment. It is my hope that Christian conversion will move beyond a salvation experience that results only in a personal piety that gets people ready for heaven. Conversion must involve people in the affairs of *this* world. If there is to be a rebirth of America, it will come only as we become engaged in those activities that affect society with the values of the Sermon on the Mount. That is why I have so strongly pled for Christians all across America to become committed to living out their faith in middle-range programs and projects designed to implement something of the agenda of the Kingdom of God.

In the praxis of trying to change the world, I found the meaning and the psychic energy that comes from reflection in action. It was in *doing* Christianity in those places where I lived and worked that the significance of my life became clear.

I am committed to global concerns such as world hunger. As a matter of fact, I am very involved in raising money for hungry children in Third World countries. But it is setting up feeding programs for the homeless in my own community that has the greatest effect on me. I believe that something must be done to curtail the demolition of the rain forest in the Amazon lest our ecological balance be permanently disturbed. I sign petitions and write to politicians to voice my concerns. But it is activities like organizing people in my own backyard to stop the use of styrofoam cups in fast-food restaurants that gets my blood running hot and stirs me to meaningful excitement.

I believe in world peace, and I am anxious to support candidates for public office who are committed to non-military solutions to world problems. But it is the reconciling of white people and black people in my own city through their work together in our tutoring program for inner-city kids that really gets me "turned on" and feeling alive.

I could go on, but I think you get the point. As important as the big issues are in the grand scheme of living on spaceship earth, it is my participation with middle-range activities wherein I am *directly* involved in what is happening and can see for myself the results of my efforts that gives my life the enlivening spirit that takes the numbness of my soul away.

It is out of my personal experiences in living out the cultural mandate of Calvinism that I have come to *feel* that my life has significance. It is in trying to change the world on the local level that I have sensed personal purpose and meaning.

Recently I heard a recording of the Statler Brothers. The lyrics of one of their songs had a haunting, tragic quality. They went like this:

> Tommy's sellin' used cars,
> Nancy's fixin' hair
> Harvey runs a groc'ry store
> And Margaret doesn't care
> Jerry drives a truck for Sears
> And Charlotte's on the make
> And Paul sells life insurance
> And part-time real estate.

And the class of '57 had its dreams
We all thought we'd change the world
With our great works and deeds; Or
Maybe we just thought the world
Would change to fit our needs
The class of '57 had its dreams.

Betty runs a trailer park
Jan sells Tupperware
Randy's in an insane ward
And Mary's on welfare;
Charley took a job with Ford
Joe took Freddy's wife
Charlotte took a millionaire
and Freddy took his life

But the class of '57 had its dreams
Ah, the class of '57 had its dreams.

Such are the tragedies of people who do not recognize
that dreams can be lived out and purposes realized right
where we live in our everyday lives. That is one reason
why these middle-range programs and projects of which
I have been speaking are so important.

A Touch of the Charismatic

In the mid-seventies I got my first strong dose of the
charismatic movement, and I liked it. Earlier in my life I
had experienced brief brushes with this dynamic expression of Christianity, but it was not until I started preaching in Pentecostal churches and at various "Jesus festi-

vals" that I began to grasp the importance of what was happening through the charismatic movement.

At first I was turned off by the emphasis that those in the charismatic movement put on "praying in tongues." I did not understand it, nor did I have any desire to get into it. It was only gradually that I came to realize that the "tongues thing" was only one small part of what the charismatic movement was all about and became open to what it could offer me.

What happened at the worship services at charismatic gatherings gave me the best understanding of the significance of this movement. Time and time again, I sensed a "power" or a "presence" come upon me in the spontaneity of charismatic worship. On many of these occasions I felt as thought I had experienced some special kind of inner release. Excitement and joy filled me, and I hungered to have these experiences more often.

At the Creation Festival, a kind of religious Woodstock that is held each year in central Pennsylvania, I experienced something of the charismatic movement without the tongues experience. The Creation Festival brings together forty thousand Christians each year for four days of contemporary Christian music and intensive preaching. Since Harry Thomas, the sponsor and promoter of the festival, is a former student of mine, I can always count on being invited to be one of the speakers.

Just before going on stage during the 1979 festival, I sensed something extra special. It was something new to me. There was a "filling of the Spirit." Call it the result of the "collective effervescence" of the crowd, as the sociologist Emile Durkheim would, or call it some kind of "psychological high" generated by the intensity of the situation. All I know is that I felt a presence. An exhilaration ran through my being, and I was lifted to a very special state of ecstasy. It has been easy ever since that experience to relate to what the seventeenth-century philosopher and scientist Blaise Pascal experienced when he wrote:

> From about half past ten in the evening
> to about a half hour after midnight—
> FIRE!
> God of Abraham, God of Isaac, God of Jacob,
> Not the God of philosophers and scholars,
> Absolute Certainty; Beyond Reason,
> Joy, Peace.
> Forgetfulness of the world and everything
> but God.
> The world has not known thee
> But I have known thee.
> Joy! Joy! Joy! Tears of Joy!

My experience also had, in my mind, a certain kinship to what John Wesley described about his Aldersgate experience:

> In the evening I went very unwillingly to a society in Aldersgate Street, where one was reading Luther's *Preface to the Epistle to the Romans*. About a quarter before nine, while he was describing the change which God works in the heart through faith in Christ, I felt my heart strangely warmed. I felt that I did trust in Christ, Christ alone for salvation; and an assurance was given me, that he had taken away my sins, even mine, and saved me from the law of

sin and death. I began to pray with all my
might for those who had in a more especial
manner dispitefully used me and persectued
me. I then testified openly to all there what I
now first felt in my heart.

This kind of experience was the charismatic movement in a form that I could embrace. And I did!

All across America, charismatic churches are growing
by leaps and bounds. Charismatic Christianity is the
fastest-growing form of Christianity around. More and
more of those who join these churches are doing so without ever speaking or praying in tongues. It is the *worship*
that attracts them. They are tired of the traditional worship of mainline denominational Christianity. People are
lured into the charismatic movement because the worship services give them a feeling of having been released
from the weight of guilt and anxiety that so often go
with living in our kind of world. All the emotions that
our consumer-oriented society promises to deliver if we
will just buy its things are more than experienced in a
full surrender to the Holy Spirit.

Consumerism may actually have helped to bring on
the charismatic experiences that are increasingly evident
throughout Christendom. The things that have been
advertised to us with the promise that they can deliver
certain emotional gratifications have failed to do so. But
as an unintended side effect the ads have made us more
aware of what is missing in our lives and have stimulat-
ed the hunger to have these emotional and spiritual
needs met. In a sense, I believe that the manipulations of
the media on behalf of consumerism have been the John
the Baptist that has prepared the way for the charismatic

movement. It is no wonder that so many are becoming neo-Pentecostal. In the worship of the charismatic movement, people are finding that which the consumeristic ads have promised but never have given.

There is an old hymn entitled "Spirit of the Living God" that describes what people are looking for in the charismatic movement. It tells of something more profound than the often sensational demonstrations of the outpouring of Spirit that are represented by praying in tongues or in healing services. Instead, this hymn speaks of taking away the dimness of the soul and of the craving for inner renewal:

> I ask no dream, no prophet's ecstasies
> No sudden rending of the veil of clay
> No angel visitant, no opening skies
> But take the dimness of my soul away.

This kind of mystical dimension to religious experience is part of the coming revival that I believe offers hope for an America numbed by consumeristic values.

I would be amiss if I did not point out that spiritual renewal is also being found through means other than the charismatic movement. There is a new interest in the kind of contemplation advocated by the likes of Thomas Merton, author of *The Seven Storey Mountain* and *Seeds of Contemplation*.* This too has played a part in generating the kind of spiritual renewal that breaks the bonds of psychic deadness that had come to mark our culture. It is true that there are other ways in which people are beginning to experience the revitalization of

---

*Thomas Merton, *The Seven Storey Mountain*, New York: Harcourt, Brace, 1948; *Seeds of Contemplation*, New York:Farrar, Straus, Giroux, 1964.

the spirit that can save America. I speak so strongly of the charismatic movement only because it is the most evident of the renewal instruments of our time and is obviously affecting the most people.

Add a Little of the Anabaptist Life-Style

Ron Sider, author of *Rich Christians in an Age of Hunger*,* teaches at Eastern Baptist Theological Seminary, a sister school to Eastern College, where I teach. We are friends who interact with fair regularity. Consequently, I have been influenced by his countercultural Anabaptist theology. At a time when I felt a need for an alternative to the dominant values and life-style of our consumer-oriented society, his views proved most attractive and helpful.

The Anabaptists have both a realism and a humility that keeps them from the triumphalism that has marked many evangelicals of the last decade. They are well aware that there are demonic forces everywhere that are not about to beat a retreat just because some zealous youth speaker calls upon those in the audience to "take over the world for Jesus." They know all too well that our society is not going to show much evidence of becoming the Kingdom of God without God Himself dramatically intervening in history.

On the other hand, Anabaptists believe that Christians are supposed to "set up" that Kingdom in the midst of this world as a kind of alternative to what is

---

*Ron Sider, *Rich Christians in an Age of Hunger*, Downers Grove, IL: Inter-Varsity, 1984.

offered by the dominant "Kingdoms of this world."

The primary spokespersons for Anabaptist theology, who include Donald Kraybill, Ron Sider, and John Howard Yoder, are being heard by Christians from groups as far-ranging and different from one another as the liberal National Council of Churches and the fundamentalist National Association of Evangelicals. Their books have become best-sellers, and their influence is conditioning the way the rest of us Christians look at the world.

Those in this Anabaptist tradition have not given up on the world. Instead, they have a different methodology for trying to change it. They contend that the most important task for Christians is to establish communities that reveal to the rest of the world the kind of society that God wants to establish here on earth. Often referred to as the Radical Reformation, they promote a life-style in community that literally adheres to the teachings of Jesus. Anabaptists are committed pacifists, zealous in ministering to the poor, and self-sacrificing servants to the oppressed and beaten down people of the world. The relief organizations of Anabaptist denominations maintain some of the most extensive and effective social service programs and economic development efforts of Christendom. They are dedicated to what they call "the servant ministries" of Jesus.

I was in a Mennonite church the Sunday after a major earthquake hit Mexico City. The pastor announced that ten members of the congregation would be leaving that very day to go to Mexico City to serve as relief workers and that they would stay on for at least a month to help the victims of the earthquake rebuild. Other members of the church were expected to fill in for these relief workers on their regular jobs, take care of the families that they left behind, and help to cover all the expenses they incurred by being away from their homes.

This incredible capacity for mobilization to meet a crisis in Mexico is just one of hundreds of ways that Anabaptists are ready to serve the world. This service is rendered in love. It is not an attempt to gain control over the social system nor is it meant to be a means of gaining political power. As a matter of fact, strict adherence to their beliefs would keep them from holding political office, being on the police force, and even voting. They want not to take over the world but to change it through loving service. They want to affect the world through what they *are* as well as what they *do*.

To use an illustration taken from the Harvard theologian Harvey Cox, Anabaptists are attempting to become God's Nova Huta. Cox explains that when the communists took over in Poland following World War II, they established what they thought would be the perfect communist city. This city, called Nova Huta, was to have ideal housing and the best possible parks and recreational facilities. It was to have excellent schools and to provide near-to-ideal work conditions. Only people who were ideologically pure communists were allowed to be citizens of Nova Huta.

The idea behind the creation of this city was that it be a demonstration of the future of Poland, set down in the midst of the present. Nova Huta was to be a sermon to the rest of Poland about what communism was attempting to create for everyone in the nation. Its primary function was to *be* all that communism was supposedly able to make a city to be. The very existence of Nova Huta was supposed to help convert the rest of Poland to a new way of life.

Anabaptists, in their traditional form, seek to do much the same thing. They want to affect the world by what they *are*. They want their lives-in-community to be so attractive that people will want to leave the ways of the world and live in accord with the will of God. They hope that the values of the Kingdom of God that they live out in their everyday lives will be so validated in the eyes of the world that those who govern its societies will endeavor to implement these values within their spheres of influence.

However, Anabaptists do not kid themselves into believing that there is no need for the Second Coming of Christ. They are convinced that while the world may be affected by the presence of communities of radically committed Christians, it will take an invasion from beyond society and from outside of history to purge the world of sin and to create the Kingdom of God on earth.

As an illustration of what is hoped for, let me tell you about the role of the French underground movement during World War II. The brave men and women in that movement were well aware of their limitations as they challenged their Nazi conquerors. They knew that they alone could not overthrow their oppressors. But in the backs of their minds, they had hope. It was a hope that a huge invasion force was being gathered across the English Channel. Furthermore, they were convinced that, in an hour that none of them knew, an invasion force would sweep onto the shores of France and join up with their ragtag army and carry them to victory. The underground movement believed that when that great day came, all that they had worked and suffered to achieve would be given new and wonderful significance. They were convinced that, in that hour, they would know that their labor had not been in vain.

In a parallel fashion, Anabaptist Christians see themselves as a kind of underground movement for God. They struggle against an awesome enemy and seem to be up against insurmountable odds. But in their efforts to bring in the Kingdom of God, they labor with hope. They believe that, in an hour known only to the Heavenly Father, their Christ will reenter human history and bring to realization the world they have been trying to create. They know that what they do in the way of social ministry is a sign of this coming event. And they believe that none of their efforts to build a Kingdom will have been in vain.

Linking Anabaptist Theology with Middle-Range Social Change

It is easy to see how such a theology can be integrated with the kind of middle-range projects that we have been talking about. Small community-based programs designed to give expression to the values of the Kingdom of God as expressed in scripture can have ultimate significance within this vision. Christian activists do not necessarily have to see the whole world change. It is enough for them to realize some small sign or evidence of the Kingdom in the projects they have taken into hand. They do not have to see Satan flee or evil disappear. It is enough for them to know that the good that they do will not be lost and that when the Lord returns, the Evil One and all of his works will be destroyed. Within the context of this optimistic view of history, there is the assurance that, though the cause of evil may prosper, it cannot retard or extinguish the work of God's people. In all of this, Anabaptists and other Christian activists agree.

Laboring to set up a feeding program for children in Haiti will not solve all the hunger problems of that country. But Christ will honor that effort and complete what it was intended to accomplish when He returns.

Building houses for poor people through Habitat for Humanity will not eliminate slums from the face of the earth. But those who build these houses can do so in the assurance that Christ will receive their hard work and, on the day of His coming, expand it into something that provides dignified living conditions for everyone.

Working to get a citywide ruling outlawing styrofoam cups at fast-food chains will not end the pollution of the environment nor do away with the impending ecological holocaust. But those who engage in such limited social action projects can look forward to a day when the Lord of History will make all things new.

Starting small businesses in Third World countries will not bring an end to poverty. But those who believe in His impending coming can do so knowing that what they do is the beginning of the end of a world of privation for some of God's children.

It is not simply that God will do something *alongside* these community-based micro projects. If that were the case, these efforts would be rendered insignificant at the Second Coming of Christ. Rather, God will take what His people have initiated and explode it into the fulfill-

ment of His will for the world. Jesus says that such small
and seemingly insignificant projects are actually *seeds*
out of which will come the full-grown manifestation of
the Kingdom of God.

My religious journey is not unusual. I am finding that
people everywhere are coming to this same kind of
Christianity. The countervailing influences of a Calvinism that takes changing the world as a mandate, a Pente-
costalism that finds spontaneity and joy in worship, and
an Anabaptist awareness that the best we can hope to
achieve before "the end" is to establish "islands of Kingdom" where the ethic of the Kingdom can be lived out
all come together to form a new version of holistic
Christianity. I believe that these three religious commitments and experiences, properly synthesized, are the
hope of the future. Together, I believe, they will create an
enlivened people who, in their living out of the gospel in
middle-range ways, will give new birth to a dying nation.

Not All Will Endure

Across America and around the world, the seeds have
been sown that even now are beginning to come to
fruition in a new breed of radical Christians. No one
seems to be able to name the prophet who sowed these
seeds, but that they *have been sown* is hard to deny.

The future is hard to figure out. We know that these
seeds of repentance and renewal will fall on different
kinds of soil. Some who receive these seeds will be
superficial in their commitment and, lacking depth, will
turn away from this radical Christianity. They will dis-
card it, as bohemians eventually turn from old fads and
look for something new.

Others will find the going too tough. They will be those who really did not count the cost of this kind of discipleship before they got started (Luke 14:25–33). They will give up and look for easier ways to live.

Still others will be seduced back into the ways of the world. After all, the sensuous allurements of the things of Babylon are more than most of us can resist. With the TV ads packaging things in erotic and egotistic wrappers, it is hard to resist buying. Before they know it, some people will be sucked back in. Instead of being committed to the justice of the Kingdom, they will be worried once again about how they can hold onto the things that they have acquired and will be concerned about how they can get more.

But every so often, and more often than one might think, there will be those individuals who get a handle on the message, realize what is involved, and go with it all the way. As the prophetic seeds take root in them, they will seek to do the works of righteousness (Matt. 5:6). In dark and forgotten places they will try to do what must be done for justice to roll down and for *shalom* to thrive. What they try to accomplish will often leave them frustrated, but they will learn from their frustrations. The people they try to serve will hurt them many times, but they will learn to see Jesus in these people anyway. What they achieve will be limited in the world's eyes, but they *will* learn how to overcome the world (John 16:33). And in the end they will bear fruit. Eventually their efforts will come to greatness. Even the seemingly little things that they do will have their rewards (Matt. 10:42). And when these people come together, they will be a presence that the world will not be able to ignore. They will be a new people who will shake the foundations of the old order. They will be a leaven in society. They will be the salt of the earth. They will be the beginning of a new Kingdom, even as the old America passes away.

And Jesus said:

> Behold, a sower went forth to sow;
> And when he sowed, some seeds fell by the way side, and the fowls came and devoured them up;
> Some fell upon stony places, where they had not much earth; and forthwith they sprung up, because they had no deepness of earth;
> And when the sun was up, they were scorched; and because they had no root, they withered away.
> And some fell among thorns; and the thorns sprung up, and choked them:
> But other fell into good ground, and brought forth fruit, some an hundredfold, some sixtyfold, some thirtyfold.
> Who hath ears to hear, let him hear.
> (Matthew 13:3–9)

I am filled with hope because there is good seed in the world. That seed has taken root and it will not be long before it yields a harvest that will bless us all.

277.3
c198

84966

LINCOLN CHRISTIAN COLLEGE AND SEMINARY